Self-Image Modification
Building Self-Esteem

D. G. Simmermacher

Health Communications, Inc.
Deerfield Beach, Florida

Donald G. Simmermacher
Albuquerque, New Mexico

First Printing, 1981
Third Printing, 1987
Revised Edition, 1989

ISBN 0-932194-09-5

Published by: Health Communications, Inc.
              Enterprise Center
              3201 S.W. 15th Street
              Deerfield Beach, FL 33442

Contents

PART ONE

SIM I — The Search For Self-Esteem

Orientation to the nature,
development and functions
of self-image and self-esteem

PREFACE

Since the manual's first publication in 1981, *Self-Image Modification (SIM) Training* has been well-received in the human service field. The program originated as an aftercare resource for persons experiencing alcohol and other drug dependencies, but over the years the program has also proven to be highly effective in dealing with many other self-image related behavioral and social problems. This edition has been reworked, broadened and expanded to assist anyone who may be interested in building a more positive self-image and self-esteem.

When I wrote the first edition of this training manual, self-image theory was not as well-known and studied as it is today. Within the last decade, considerably more has been written on the subject (see Bibliography). I have, therefore, incorporated more current material and information regarding self-image and self-esteem in this edition. Further, in order to have this training manual both more readable and teachable, I have tried to present the material in an organized and systematic manner that will allow the reader to translate self-image theory into practical application. The main objective of the SIM Training program is to provide training-group experiences to assist participants in acquiring a more positive self-image and self-esteem through the process of self-actualization and human growth.

SIM Training utilizes a systems approach designed to actualize human potential and enhance self-esteem. The training manual is divided into two parts — SIM I and SIM II. SIM I, entitled "The Search For Self-Esteem," deals with an orientation to the nature, development and functions of self-image and self-esteem in everyday life. SIM II, entitled "Self-Image Modification Training," describes a model to the training-group process. SIM II also explains and illustrates each of the six functions used in this system model. In addition a self-image inventory and group participant tracking forms, as well as a variety of group exercises, are available as a means of guiding the group through the system functions.

It is important to note that each one of the six system functions is designed so that the individual function builds on the other, and thereby provides a logical and orderly process for human growth and change.

The group exercises and activities found in SIM II are designed primarily for use with reasonably healthy, well-functioning people who are interested in better achieving their potential and building self-esteem. Though not intended to be the equivalent or substitute for conventional psychotherapy or mental health treatment, the educational experience can strengthen self-esteem, interpersonal skills and potentials for human growth in a supportive training-group setting.

INTRODUCTION — SIM I

One of the first concepts involved in influencing the enhancement of self-esteem is the process of self-actualization. Self-actualization is a term best identified with the noted psychologist and author, Abraham Maslow. He is well-known for his theory of self-actualization, and no attempt will be made here to review his work in detail. The basic principle of self-actualization is that all human beings are motivated by a common set of fundamental values or needs. The goal of human striving and accomplishment is to "become the best that one can be," continually working to achieve one's potential.

The self-actualization needs identified by Maslow are related to each other in the form of a hierarchy of lower to higher level needs and are listed as follows:

(1) physiological needs
(2) safety or security needs
(3) love, affection and belonging needs
(4) self-esteem and self-worth needs
(5) the need for self-actualization.

While the lower maintenance needs are basic to human life and survival, the higher level human needs of self-esteem and self-actualization are of greatest concern in realizing human potential.

Self-esteem includes the need for self-acceptance, self-respect, self-confidence, self-trust, self-reliance and self-worth. The need to like, respect and value one's self is necessary for one to experience meaning, purpose and fulfillment in life. Building self-esteem is perhaps the most important function of the human growth process. Self-esteem is to the mind as food is to the

5

body, and all human beings need self-esteem for both physical and psychological well-being.

Self-actualization means to experience human growth through personal effort and action. Self-actualization is defined as achieving in action. All people have a need to work toward attaining their potential, to develop talents and to achieve personal goals. Self-actualization may be thought of as achieving self-fulfillment and self-realization through living one's values and arriving at personally selected life goals. Every individual has both potentials and human limitations. Each human being is endowed with unique aptitudes, talents, abilities and natural inclinations. Not everyone may be able to become a successful poet, musician, artist, professional athlete and so forth; but everyone does have other potential talents and abilities that can be developed more fully. People will never become fully self-actualized or exhaust all their human potentials, but they can continually move from self-defeating to self-actualizing behavior.

It should be recognized that achieving potential does not mean achieving perfection. Striving for excellence is one thing while expecting to achieve perfection is quite another. Perfectionists are unable to acquire self-esteem because they are never good enough in their own eyes. We are all imperfect beings in an imperfect world, and we all have the ability of achieving self-esteem as capable and worthwhile human beings.

CHAPTER ONE

Who Is The Enemy?

*"A person who doubts himself is like a man who would enlist in the
ranks of his enemies and bear arms against himself."*

Alexandre Dumas

Who is the enemy? We carry him around with ourselves wherever we go. He
robs us of our dignity, self-worth, hopes and freedom. He destroys our potential
for happiness, fulfillment and human growth. He stands as a barrier between
ourselves and other human beings. Who is the enemy? The enemy resides in
all of us to some degree. The enemy is our own negative self-image and low
self-esteem.

Self-Image

Our self-image can be our best friend or worst enemy depending on its
strength or weakness. Over 25 years in the human services field has convinced
me that the greatest social problem of many present-day human beings is the
inability to acquire a positive self-image and self-esteem. This fact is reflected
in the alarming rate of suicide, especially among today's young people. It is
further revealed in the millions of people who become alcoholics or become
dependent on other widely used mind-altering chemicals. Low self-esteem
appears to be a causal factor in the loss of meaning and purpose experienced
in people's work, personal and family relationships, and leisure-time activities.

Positive Identity And Self-Esteem

The need for a positive identity and self-esteem is common to all human beings. This need includes the fundamental achievement of self-acceptance, self-respect, self-confidence, self-reliance and self-worth. Knowing and believing that our self-image can change for the better is the first step in the human growth process. It is no exaggeration to state that acquiring a positive self-image and authentic self-esteem is essential for self-worth and healthy personal adjustment.

One of the leading authorities and authors on the subject of self-esteem, Dr. Nathaniel Branden, emphasizes the importance of self-esteem in everyday life in the following quote from his book entitled, *How To Raise Your Self-Esteem:*

How we feel about ourselves crucially affects virtually every aspect of our experience, from the way we function at work, in love, in sex, to the way we operate as parents, to how high in life we are likely to rise. Our responses to the happenings in our everyday life are shaped by who and what we think we are. I believe that self-esteem is the key to success or failure. Self-esteem has another more important value — it also holds the key to understanding ourselves and other people. I cannot think of a single psychological problem that is not traceable to the problem of poor self-concept. Positive self-esteem is a cardinal requirement of a fulfilling life.

The purpose of the rest of this part of the training manual is to shed more light on the nature, development and functions of self-image and self-esteem in your everyday life.

CHAPTER TWO

Self-Image Is Learned

Self-image (how people think and feel about themselves as persons) is a product of learning. One is not born with a self-image, but rather self-image is acquired through social interaction and social responses. How you think and feel about yourself as a person is learned in the same way you learned to speak the language of your parents. Since self-image is learned, it logically follows that our image of self can be unlearned, relearned or changed. A positive self-image can be taught. Self-image can be thought of as a subject of study much as one would study language, history, biology, mathematics and so forth. Clearly then, learning to have a positive self-image and authentic self-esteem should be taught both at home and in school.

Positive Self-Image

Unfortunately, our social institutions, such as family, school, church, etc., in general are not doing a good job in educating our youth in learning how to develop a positive self-image. Having a positive self-image and self-esteem requires the owning of one's assets and potentials while also being realistic about one's liabilities and human limitations.

To acknowledge one's good qualities and abilities is often considered a form of conceit, boasting or bragging. However, nothing could be further from the truth. There is a great deal of difference between healthy self-acceptance and bragging based on false pride. Owning one's true potentials and assets is really an expression of authentic self-awareness. A person with a positive image of self does not resort to bravado or being a "grandstander." Conceit and self-centeredness are a result of a negative image of self, not a positive one. Bragging and acting the "big shot" is really a form of pseudo or false self-esteem. Those who truly own their potentials and assets do not have a need to brag or call attention to themselves. They simply recognize their positive attributes while also keeping an eye on their human limitations.

Having a sense of self-reliance and self-trust requires that people know their true selves. Just as you would not give blanket trust to one you did not know, you would not do the same with yourself. Self-trust is essential to achieving self-actualization and human growth.

In the words of Ralph Waldo Emerson, *"Self-trust is the first secret of success."*

Narcissistic Pride

Narcissistic pride is sometimes confused with positive self-acceptance and self-love. It is a common error to confuse healthy versus unhealthy self-love. Narcissism is not healthy self-love but is symptomatic of self-rejection and self-hate. Narcissism involves an exaggerated or excessive preoccupation with self to the exclusion of others. This form of egotistical behavior is an attempt to gain reassurance — to compensate for a negative self-image and low self-esteem. Grandiosity is another common term used for this self-image problem. Grandiosity is an example of trying to own what one doesn't have rather than owning what one does truly possess. As indicated, people with a positive self-image are willing to own their potentials and assets while recognizing and accepting their liabilities and limitations.

In the words of Hugh Prather, *"Until I accept my faults, I certainly doubt my virtues."*

Negative Self-Image

Negative self-image people usually dwell on their frailties and faults instead of their strengths and potentials. They often tend to distort small failures and imperfections into overwhelming feelings of failure and inferiority. Positive self-image people, on the other hand, do not see themselves as being either superior or inferior to others. They tend to display an attitude of humanistic equality, i.e., all people are equal as human beings.

As Eleanor Roosevelt stated, *"No one can make you feel inferior without your consent."*

No man can be cheated of his human dignity unless he cheats himself. We cheat ourselves by failing to believe in ourselves, and to maintain dignity and self-worth. Self-confidence and self-trust are based on self-knowledge and total self-acceptance as a capable and worthwhile human being. Self-acceptance and self-worth are the best insurance against making wrong choices and against experiencing personal failure. Self-respect is the most valuable possession we can own. Someone may take our money, property or other possessions, but only we can rob ourselves of a positive self-image and self-esteem.

Riches Of Positive Self-Image

If you keep your positive self-image and self-esteem, no matter what other things you may lose in life, you will still be rich in many ways. Having the gift of self-acceptance, self-reliance and self-esteem provides one with abundant resources and opportunities to live a rewarding and fulfilling life. As indicated, those with a positive image of self are not smug or boastful, but neither are they handicapped by thoughts and feelings of self-depreciation.

As Allen Fromme points out in his, *Our Troubled Selves,* there are both winners and losers in life, and very often the difference is not one of talent but one of belief in one's self. It may be hard to classify ourselves as either winners or losers because most of us probably fall somewhere in between these two extremes. As Fromme says, our self-image is not all that clear-cut. His definition of a positive self-image makes this point when he writes:

A person who has an adequate conception of himself is not sad, but he does not have to be deliriously happy. He is not unacceptable to others in his own eyes, but he does not feel that he has to be a social lion. He is not pessimistic but his optimism is not unbridled. He is neither foolhardy nor free of specific fears. He is not incapable of being wrong, but he is not always wrong. He realizes that he is not the outstanding success of all times, nor is he a perennial failure. Above all, the person with a good self-image is capable of love and understanding.

CHAPTER THREE

Being In Becoming

"Being in becoming" is a humanistic term that is closely related to self-actualization. Some say **being** (existing) is more important in the building of a positive self-image than **becoming** (achieving potential). Just being or existing is sufficient for self-worth and self-esteem. I tend to disagree. I believe a positive self-image is a product of self-actualization and human growth. Being a person implies becoming a person — being in process or "being in becoming."

Self-Responsibility

This process of becoming requires a sense of self-responsibility. As William C. Shutz states, *"Man's self-concept is enhanced when he takes responsibility for himself."* Responsibility is defined as the ability to respond. We almost always have the choice of how to respond to life situations. We are creatures of choice. Responsibility, of course, requires freedom to choose. People must accept responsibility for their own lives and the fulfillment of needs. Individuals are responsible for finding their own meaning and purpose in life. I believe when the concept of nonresponsibility is rejected, the dignity and self-worth of human beings will be increased. Responsibility, or the ability to respond, is the basis for personal dignity and self-worth.

Social Responsibility

Achieving a positive image of self and self-esteem also requires a sense of social responsibility. Enhancing self-esteem and achieving potential should not be pursued at the expense of others. For people to achieve their needs by depriving others of their rightful needs is to perform an immoral act. There is overwhelming evidence that positive self-image people treat others with fairness, respect, kindness and dignity while it is those with a negative image of self who tend to be more likely to mistreat or be abusive toward others. It is also known that self-esteem is enhanced when one takes the opportunity to help and be of service to others. The need for a sense of social responsibility is well expressed in the following words of Etienne de Grellet: *"I expect to pass through life but once. If, therefore, there be any kindness I can show or any good thing I can do to any fellow being, let me do it now . . . as I shall not pass this way again."*

Development Of Self-Image

At this point, it should be clear to you, the reader, that a positive self-image must be developed. It does not grow by itself. No one can stop us from achieving a more positive self-image if we are truly committed and are willing to make the necessary effort to do so. A positive self-image and self-esteem begin with authentic self-acceptance and self-reliance. As indicated, self-image is always subject to change despite the past. No single event or person can determine the level of one's self-esteem — it develops over time and is constantly subject to change at any age. As Virginia Satir so aptly said, *"Learning to value oneself, having high self-esteem, having self-confidence can happen to anyone despite the past."*

It should be clear that no one ever has a totally positive or totally negative self-image. Our image of self is often situational and cannot be measured on any absolute scale. We all feel confident about some things and shaky about others. We all have our individual human strengths and limitations. It is important to remember, however, that our feeling of self-worth can be enhanced through the achievement of our own unique potentialities — by becoming what we can become. Self-acceptance and personal growth are both linked to the search for higher levels of self-fulfillment. This drive for human growth and self-actualization is common to all human beings, and we can all share in the lifelong process of "being in becoming."

CHAPTER FOUR

Know Thyself

The self-image comprises all of the beliefs that we hold regarding the mental picture we have of ourselves as a person. These beliefs can be quite accurate or extremely distorted. The closer our image of self matches our true or real self, the more able we are to deal with the world of reality. On the other hand, when our self-image is not congruent with our real self, we can experience what psychologists call identity confusion or self-alienation. Almost all mental health professionals agree that the ability to know one's real self is a basic requirement of good mental stability and personal adjustment. The Greek philosopher Socrates left us with sound words of wisdom, *"Know thyself, know your strengths and your weaknesses, your potentials and limitations; take stock of yourself."*

An accurate awareness of self can be a true asset in allowing us to determine our real needs, values and life goals. Authentic self-knowledge is essential for the acquisition of a positive self-image and self-esteem. We must think about our potentials and limitations if we are to experience personal growth and self-actualization. This is the first step in the self-image modification process.

Self-Image Inventory

A way to gain insight regarding our potentials and limitations is to list them on a self-image inventory. List the traits we value in ourselves and the skills we are good at on one half of the inventory sheet. Factors to be considered in this area could include such things as sensitivity, creativity, common sense, good habits, natural ability, integrity, good health, etc. On the other side of the inventory sheet, list those characteristics that are seen as personal liabilities or limitations. We must remember that it is okay and realistic for all human beings to have limitations, such as laziness, bad habits, bad temper, moodiness, antisocial tendencies, poor problem-solving skills, etc.

As a former vocational education counselor, I am sensitive to the importance of knowing our potentials, limitations, aptitudes and natural inclinations. I have seen many students who decided to attend college or a vocational school who had no idea of their area of concentration. As a late academic bloomer myself (beginning my college studies in my early 30s), I began my college experience with little or no idea of what major field of study would be best suited to my interests, aptitudes and abilities. To be successful in the achievement of future goals, it is helpful to know as much as we can about ourselves and the world we live in. We must be aware of our capabilities as well as our human limitations. Personal strength acknowledgment is particularly important in successfully tapping potentials leading to human growth and positive self-image change.

Group exercises to enhance self-knowledge and self-awareness can be found under the function, *Conceptualize Self,* SIM II, Chapter Twenty-Six.

CHAPTER FIVE

Statement Of Philosophy

The dictionary partially defines philosophy as "the statement of values by which one lives." A statement of philosophy is a personal disclosure of what one believes to be true regarding the meaning and purpose of life. It is a declaration of what one believes to be true about self and the world of reality.

Value System

Self-realization requires that all human beings seek some value or system of beliefs to which they can commit themselves. Belief in a value system serves as a guide to our personal decisions, actions and behavior. Personal growth requires that we adopt a philosophy or value system that can lead to rational planning and thoughtful action. It is through one's value system that one is able to achieve personal growth. This kind of knowledge can assist in giving one a sense of direction and purpose in life. Translating one's philosophy or values into specific and meaningful goals is essential for personal growth and self-actualization.

Individuals must choose their own beliefs and values that guide their actions and determine goals. They are responsible for identifying and examining their own basic values underlying their own life goals and objectives. This is often a hard lesson for people to accept. It is human nature for us to want to impose our values on others. It is often very difficult to have the patience and tolerance to let others choose their own values and beliefs. This is particularly true of people in authority or power positions such as parents, teachers, work supervisors, etc. We all know of people with certain political or religious ideologies

17

who are quite willing, even eager, to tell others how to live their lives. The sociological term, ethnocentrism, implies the belief in the superiority of one's own cultural or ethnic group values over the values of outsiders. The implication here is that I will only accept you when you become willing to adopt and adhere to my beliefs and values. Until you do so, I will reject you. One does not have to look far to see the social problems that this kind of dogmatic and rigid thinking causes in the world today.

Value Compromise

Another important factor related to self-image and values is that of value compromise. Value compromise can be either positive or negative depending on the situation. For instance, to compromise one's moral or ethical values can result in an assault on one's self-esteem. We have all experienced this problem at one time or another. Negative feelings, such as guilt and remorse, can come about if we compromise our values of decency, justice, honesty or fair play. Because of our irrational or distorted thinking, we sometimes can easily become the victims of unearned guilt. Remember the saying, "We follow our knows." We may sometimes blindly follow the questionable values or beliefs of others because of a lack of self-confidence to think for ourselves or to ask the right questions. People with a positive self-image are neither blind followers or compulsive rebels, but rather they demonstrate the self-image strength to be assertive and to take charge of their own lives.

Value compromise can also be seen as a strength rather than a weakness. In my experience as a marriage counselor, I am frequently confronted with the value conflicts going on in a marriage. Both parties, for instance, may have value conflicts on how to spend their money, on how to raise their children, or on how to spend their leisure-time activities. In order to establish a cooperative and more harmonious relationship, the willingness for one or both parties to compromise values should be obvious. Being too "hard headed" or stubborn to consider value compromise would prevent a successful reconciliation.

Relationship Between Self-Esteem And Values

The point has been successfully made that there is a significant relationship between self-esteem and values, and it is up to each individual to consider the importance of values clarification in the human growth process. We can always choose our own values, but we cannot always choose the consequences of these value choices. After a number of years working with alcoholics, I have learned that alcoholics will not maintain sobriety until they truly value sobriety. It is difficult, if not impossible, to will ourselves over something we truly desire or value. Healthy individuals are aware of their values and the forces that shape them, and are able to control these forces as well.

Our self-selected values are vital to the development of a unifying philosophy of life. Our values can provide a healthy outlook for the future and become the foundation for our hopes, aspirations and dreams. Values provide the corner-stone of life and give us our very purpose for living. The German philosopher, Nietzsche, captured the importance of life values when he said, *"He who has a why to live can bear with almost any how."*

Human growth may be defined as self-change in a valued direction. The most important aspect of the growth process is the translation of values into life goals and objectives. The pursuit of life goals never ends and can be regarded as central to one's personal identity and self-esteem. The identification of goals and objectives will be covered in the next section.

Group exercises for the function, *Statement Of Philosophy,* can be found in SIM II, Chapter Twenty-Seven.

CHAPTER SIX

Identify Goals And Objectives

After having completed the awareness steps of self-knowledge and values clarification, it becomes necessary to put this information into action. It is now time to translate your potentials and values into goals and objectives. Determine what specific, realistic, meaningful and measurable goals you want to achieve. Establish goal priorities and then develop a plan of action for goal attainment.

Relationship Between Goals And Objectives

It is important to understand the relationship between goals and objectives while also being able to distinguish between the different meanings of these two terms. A goal may be defined in more general terms than an objective. A goal is a statement of what one wishes to accomplish, acquire or achieve. The goal of becoming a more happy person is an example of a common goal. An objective, on the other hand, is a specific action or activity one must take in order to achieve the goal. An objective is a statement of what one must do in order to make the goal an accomplished reality. Objectives need to be stated as behavioral objectives. That is, an objective must be stated in a specific way that will allow it to become measurable.

For instance, in the example of the goal of happiness, one must identify the specific actions one needs to take in achieving happiness. Perhaps the loss of 10 pounds of body weight within the next month would result in personal gratification and happiness. This loss of 10 pounds within a month becomes the objective since this accomplishment is clearly specific and easily measurable. All one needs to do in this case is to get on the scale at the beginning of the designated time period and again at the end, to see if the weight loss goal has been met.

Another way to distinguish between goals and objectives is to consider the well-known ancient Chinese proverb, *"A journey of a thousand miles begins with a single step."* The thousand-mile journey is the general goal while the first step, which is necessary measurable action one must take to reach the goal, may be viewed as a specific objective.

Though it is true that some goals may not be as easy to translate into behavioral objectives as the two examples just given, all goals need to be placed within observable, measurable time boundaries. Some other related criteria should also be considered regarding the establishment of goals and objectives.

Considerations For Successful Goal Achievement

Specific Goals

Goals need to be stated in specific terms. Goals such as "I'm going to be a better person" or "I'm going to become a happier person" are not sufficient because they are too general. General goals tend to be vague and nebulous. In order to identify steps in achieving goals, the goals must be defined and stated in more specific terms. Failure to achieve goals is often due to the failure to identify specific objectives.

Realistic Goals

Goals must be in keeping with our potentials and limitations. Setting goals too high invites failure while setting goals too low can result in settling for second best. Goals must be realistic in keeping with individual potentials and resources, and should be aimed at the elimination of self-defeating behaviors.

Meaningful Goals

A goal that is not considered valuable or one that has no practical application to the individual will be viewed as meaningless and not worthy of personal effort. Individuals must first clarify values before they can translate values to goals and objectives. Goals become a way of allowing people to live their values.

Measurable Goals

Goals need to be measurable so that people can identify if and when they have been accomplished. Nonmeasurable goals can leave individuals in the dark about their own progress toward goal achievement. Goals that do not meet the criteria of measurability can be difficult, if not impossible, to reach.

Plan Of Action

"Failing to plan is planning to fail." A well thought out plan of action is usually necessary in order to become sufficiently motivated toward goal achievement. Identifying a clear path to a desired goal can increase efforts in attaining the goal. Planning keeps people oriented toward the future and allows them to gauge both short- and long-term goal efforts and accomplishments.

Goal Commitment

The relationship between values and goal commitment is obvious. The more value placed on the goal, the more commitment people are likely to make toward it. A half-hearted goal commitment will result in a half-hearted effort. Commitment is best achieved through self-selected and nonimposed goals. Commitment to working on goals that have not been voluntarily chosen will be a weak commitment at best.

In the human growth process, it is essential that every human being identify and work to achieve self-selected goals. As Gordon Allport states in his classic book *Becoming*, all healthy human beings have a continuous need for goal setting and achievement. Allport writes, *"The possession of goals distinguishes the human being from the animal, the adult from the child, and, in many cases, the healthy personality from the sick."* Once goals and objectives have been identified, personal effort to carry them out becomes the next step.

Group exercises for the function, *Define Personal Goals And Objectives,* can be found in SIM II, Chapter Twenty-Eight.

CHAPTER SEVEN

Goal-Effort Evaluation

In giving much thought to the self-evaluation process of goal efforts, I use the PHD acronym of goal sabotage. The **P** stands for **procrastination**, the **H** for **habits**, and the **D** for **dependencies**. In this section we will begin by looking at each one of these factors that can stifle our goal efforts.

Procrastination

The dictionary defines procrastination as follows: "To put off doing something until a future time, to postpone or delay endlessly." Procrastination involves specific goals or tasks that are considered important but which we fail to start. There are many reasons or excuses for procrastinating that cannot be completely covered here, but let's take a look at several of the most common ones.

Unclear Goals And Objectives

Sometimes people procrastinate because they are confused or uncertain about their goals and objectives. They may be confused so that they have no idea about how to start goal action or effort. This could very well be a signal that the individual has failed to meet one or more of the successful goal achievement considerations listed in Chapter Six, *Identify Goals And Objectives.*

Fear Of Failure

People very often procrastinate because they believe they may fail at the task. Procrastination can be a way of protecting oneself from the fear of making a mistake. This is particularly true of someone who suffers from "failure identity" or who may be a compulsive perfectionist. Personal growth requires the willingness to take some risks.

Fear Of Success

This may sound like a strange paradox, but in reality it is just the opposite of fear of failure. To the degree that our achievements and successes in life surpass our self-confidence and feelings of self-reliance, we may experience vulnerability and increased threats to our self-image. Fear of getting more responsibility as we move up the ladder of success can decrease our motivation to seek new accomplishments.

Boredom

Boredom can clearly stifle our motivation toward goal achievement. Failure to take interest in our daily tasks can result in lethargic behavior. Someone who fails to achieve job satisfaction, for instance, may find it hard to generate the energy and enthusiasm needed in being a task-oriented and productive worker.

Inadequate Goal Reward

Failure to anticipate sufficient reward for our goal efforts can influence the tendency to procrastinate. Spending a dollar's worth of energy for a penny return can make our efforts seem worthless. Sometimes we may need to provide our own rewards as a means of experiencing goal-effort satisfaction.

Fatigue

Both physical and mental fatigue can result in procrastination. We may be too tired to continue pursuing our goal efforts. Lacking the physical or mental energy to take on a new task or endeavor may cause us to put off today what we can do tomorrow.

In generating this suggested list of reasons for procrastination, it is apparent that there are too many possibilities to attempt to cover them all here. (I have, therefore, decided to procrastinate on this task and perhaps save it for another book.) It is sufficient to state that procrastination can keep us from realizing our potential and fulfilling our goals regardless of what excuses or reasons we may give ourselves for putting off tasks.

Habits

Habits, the second factor leading to goal sabotage, are actions or behavior that one takes automatically or unconsciously through frequent repetition.

Habits, of course, are not always bad. We can have many good habits that can assist us in leading efficient and productive lives. Some good habits can eliminate the unnecessary expenditure of time and energy in our daily activities. Negative personal habits can, however, be a deterrent in the goal-effort accomplishment and achievement process. Some habits are helpful in that they may be effective timesavers while others may be most counterproductive. The breaking of negative or unwanted habits can be a hard and difficult process. Part of the function of goal-effort evaluation then is to consider personal habits that may stifle self-improvement or work against fulfillment of our human growth goals and objectives.

Dependencies

The last, but not least, of the goal sabotage factors is that of dependencies. Negative self-image people tend to believe they are victims in life and frequently turn to others because of feelings that they are unable to fend for themselves. Dependency is a condition that deprives dependent people of their freedom to choose their own course of action leading toward personal growth and self-fulfillment. To be overly dependent on external sources means to give up one's freedom in problem-solving and need-fulfillment activities.

Human beings in their infancy state are totally dependent on others for their survival and maintenance needs. All throughout life human beings must form dependent or interdependent relationships with significant others in order to fulfill the need for love, acceptance, recognition and belonging. As a social being, "No man is an island" and remains dependent on others for social need gratification. A certain degree of dependency can be a positive factor in human relationships, but neurotic or parasitic dependency can be most destructive. A love that feeds on dependency will destroy itself. Excessive dependency can be a serious and crippling handicap in achieving our desired goals and objectives. (More will be said on self-image and dependency in SIM I, Chapters Eight and Seventeen.)

Total Self-Acceptance

Self-evaluation of personal goal efforts must always include total self-acceptance. Total self-acceptance is absolutely essential for self-esteem. In the pursuit of identified personal goals, one must avoid self-condemnation if goals are not being met. Failure to achieve goals can mean several things. Perhaps the goals were not realistic in terms of potential or resources. It may be decided that the goals are not sufficiently valuable or significantly meaningful.

Unsuccessful realization of goals may require a new strategy or plan of action. A stronger personal commitment to working on goals or even goal modification may be necessary. For people to benefit from goal-effort evaluation, it is important that they always continue to accept themselves as worthwhile and capable individuals with the necessary potential for human growth and positive change. Maintaining an attitude of self-respect and a good opinion of self in the goal-effort evaluation process will provide the courage and tenacity to pursue goals regardless of obstacles, temporary setbacks or difficult circumstances. Through self-confidence and self-reliance, we can turn our stumbling blocks into stepping-stones.

Group exercises for goal-effort monitoring can be found under the function, *Evaluate Self,* in SIM II Chapter Twenty-Nine.

CHAPTER EIGHT

Development Of A Positive Self-Image And Self-Esteem

In an ever-changing and depersonalized world, we must struggle to find our own identity and self-esteem. Each of us must make a conscious effort to find our own niche in life and to achieve our human potential. We must build sufficient self-confidence and self-reliance to weather life's storms and to ward off assaults to our self-image. Blows to our self-respect and self-esteem can heal more slowly than do bodily injuries and can leave scars that are even more lasting. Acquiring and maintaining a high level of self-confidence and self-regard are essential if we wish to keep developing, expanding and growing as a person.

Self-Image Changes Are Gradual And Take Time

Overnight self-image changes are extremely rare. We may, on occasion, experience sudden flashes of insight that promote change; but most changes in our self-concept are gradual and take time. Our self-image is a product of social learning. It is learned throughout our total life and should never be considered a completed fact. Our self-image is subject to development and change as long as we live. This is the most exciting and optimistic fact about self-image — knowing that self-image growth and self-esteem enhancement are always possible at any age no matter what our past experiences have been or how old we become.

Self-Awareness And Values Clarification

The search for self-esteem best begins with self-awareness and clarification of our own values. Our choice of self-determined values gives guidance and

29

meaning to our life. Through self-fulfilling activity, through the working to achieve our values and goals, we acquire authentic self-esteem. Self-selected values and goal achievement are the most important factors in our quest for self-esteem. Measuring ourselves against others' values and goals can blind us to our own inner strengths and human potentials. A self-image that depends on external sources for recognition and approval is a fragile image at best. Relying on self-approval and self-acceptance everywhere except within ourselves can make us feel insecure, inadequate and extremely vulnerable. Even though our personal successes and accomplishments may be recognized and admired by others, we may still look on ourselves as a failure. Failing to acknowledge our own achievements and accomplishments can leave us feeling like a fraud. As Nathaniel Branden states in his book *How To Raise Your Self-Esteem*, *"To attain 'success' without attaining positive self-esteem is to be condemned to feeling like an imposter anxiously awaiting exposure."*

In the development of a positive self-image and self-esteem, it is important that we maintain a self-directed initiative in achieving our potential — that we seek out our values and goals for self-realization. To be other-directed means to become dependent on others for affirmation to our own self-worth and self-esteem. Comparing ourselves to others can result in diminished self-regard. Insight about the struggle to develop our own unique identity is given by e.e. cummings in the following:

> . . . to be nobody — but yourself — in a world that is doing its best, night and day, to make you everybody else — means to fight the hardest battle which any human being can fight, and never stop fighting.

Each of us must assume responsibility for achieving our own potential and self-esteem. In the book, *Who Are You?* Raymond Gale reminds us of our need for self-directed ways to affirm our personal identity, values and goals:

> The self-directing individual, who has discovered a meaningful personal identity, is independent of outside influences in the sense that he has thought out his own values and has decided on his own goals . . . He may identify himself closely with other people and work hard to achieve group goals, but he remains aware of himself as an individual whose personal identity is something quite apart from any group. He is not afraid to be different if "being different" means acting in the light of his own values, knowledge and experience. Only as an individual approaches this kind of independence does continuing growth and self-actualization become possible. In short, he has the courage to be, to experience vitally his own existence and becoming.

To look for self-acceptance and self-esteem outside of ourselves will cause us to fail in the search. We are the author of our own self-esteem.

CHAPTER NINE

Self-Ideal And Self-Realization

The **self-image** is the picture we have of ourselves — how we think and feel about ourselves as persons. **Self-esteem** means that one has a positive sense of self-worth and self-acceptance as a person. The **self-ideal** involves what we would like to be or become as a person. Generally speaking, the wider the distance between our self-image and our self-ideal, the lower will be our self-esteem. Though our self-image, self-esteem and self-ideal can be considered separate components, these self-functions are highly interrelated and interdependent. This multiple, yet unified nature of the self, is well expressed in the following short verse by John Masefield:

And there were three men
Went down the road
As down the road went he
The man they saw, the man he was
And the man he wanted to be.

The ideal self is the image a person has of the kind of person he or she wants to be. As Raymond Gale states, *"When the ideal self is founded upon a realistic assessment of one's own capacities and limitations, it can serve as a compass to guide the individual's behavior, his long-range goals and his planning and implementation of aspirations — a road map for his effective living."*

Relationship Between Self-Ideal And Self-Realization

The relationship between the self-ideal and self-realization is quite apparent. The self-ideal serves as a foundation for our personal values and philosophy of life — our aspirations and desired life achievements. Our self-ideal provides a standard or norm by which we measure our own human growth and self-realization. When we believe we do not measure up to our self-ideal, we can develop feelings of personal disappointment and self-rejection.

It is most important, therefore, that our self-ideal be both realistic and achievable. Unrealistically high aspirations can result in failure and defeat, whereas unrealistically low aspirations can deprive us of the opportunity of achieving our true potential. It is also true that even though our self-image and self-ideal should be in close proximity, they should not be identical. Self-realization and human growth comprise a continuous life process, and our self-ideal should always be such that it provides the motivation and incentive to strive for personal achievement, growth and self-realization.

As indicated, our self-ideal assists in providing a unified value system and philosophy of life. It is our self-selected value system that determines our life goals and objectives. People who work to achieve their values and goals will usually enjoy a high level of self-esteem and feelings of self-worth. When we act in accordance with our realistic self-ideal, the sense of a positive identity tends to be reinforced. An unrealistic, rigid and inflexible self-expectation, however, can produce a kind of "tyrannical" self-ideal that can lead to anxiety, stress, apprehension and guilt if not achieved. A self-ideal demanding perfectionism or faultless behavior is programmed to fail. In his book *Personal Adjustment*, Sidney Jourard makes the following statement regarding the self-ideal's influence on human conduct and behavior:

> In view of the continual self-evaluation which goes on during a person's life, it should be apparent that when the self-ideal is violated by the person's conduct — when he does not behave as he believes he should — he will hate himself or believe he is a failure, a sinner or just plain "no good." If he behaves as he should, he will experience self-esteem and believe that he is a worthwhile, likeable, acceptable person.

An authentic and reasonably accurate self-ideal can serve as a standard or target for self-realization. Failure to achieve one's self-ideal should never result in feelings of hopelessness or discouragement. The self-ideal should always be seen as a guideline to self-realization and not an absolute indicator of success or failure as a human being. Through self-realization and the achievement of our human potential, we enhance self-sufficiency and self-esteem. By working to reach our self-ideal, we gain a greater sense of self-acceptance, self-pride and self-respect.

CHAPTER TEN

Protective Defenses And Resistance To Change

*"A child's life is like a piece of paper on which
every passerby leaves a mark."*

Ancient Chinese proverb

It is true that many traits and beliefs about the self can become fairly rigid and fixed during the formative years of life; but, as stated earlier, self-image change is possible at any age. Then why do we tend to often resist change? Fear of change is the answer to this question. We are creatures of habit, are often afraid to take reasonable risks, and find it difficult to adapt to change or new and unfamiliar situations. We may feel compelled to stick to the familiar even when doing so may be highly self-destructive and self-defeating.

People with a negative self-image tend to rely heavily on the familiar and status quo to maintain their sense of identity. Sigmund Freud referred to this as the "repetition compulsion." Sometimes we would rather cling to old and unsatisfying jobs, or continue to stay in toxic and destructive relationships rather than risk change. (This may often be due to exaggerated security or dependency needs.) Staying the way we are may be painful but it is seen as the path of least resistance. In order to experience positive change, we must be willing to take risks. Irrational fears can destroy our opportunities to gain self-confidence and self-esteem. The fear of giving up old values and beliefs that provide predictability and consistency can sometimes stifle 'he potential for positive growth and change.

One of the most common obstacles to constructive change is the overuse of self-image defenses. Maslow referred to these exaggerated defenses as pseudo or artificial need fulfillment. Our protective defenses can become isolating walls. The excessive use of self-image defenses can distort reality, and make us prisoners of our own irrational fears and erroneous beliefs. The purpose of a defense mechanism is not just to protect us from others but to defend our own fragile feelings of self-worth and self-esteem. The excessive and exaggerated use of defenses can block self-awareness and self-realization. In such a case, the cost of maintaining our self-esteem may be purchased at a very high price. When defenses are used to screen out unpleasant thoughts and to maintain the status quo, healthy self-image changes can be forfeited.

People with a negative self-image tend to use self-image defenses in a continuous, exaggerated and rigid manner. The normal or rational use of these defense mechanisms can help us control those feelings and thoughts that pose a threat to our image of self. This may be thought of as a healthy and adaptive use of defense mechanisms. The irrational overuse of defense mechanisms causes them to become counterproductive in the human growth process. It should be kept in mind that defense mechanisms are used to screen out unpleasant thoughts and feelings that threaten self-esteem, and that self-image defenses will be used as long as they are needed. To destructively confront or criticize people for their use of self-image defenses can have a harmful effect. When we realize that others see through our protective defenses, we may feel very threatened and frightfully vulnerable. One will not likely overcome the need for self-image defenses until such time that one attains the self-image strength to do so.

The use of self-image defense mechanisms, such as compensation, denial of reality, fantasy, projection, rationalization, repression, displacement, self-pity, etc., can give a good clue as to the individual's self-image strength or weakness. Self-image defenses can serve a functional purpose in assisting one in making positive adjustments in everyday life. Most people do not possess a positive self-image to the extent they can completely abandon the use of these defenses, but overusing them can be destructive and function as countergrowth factors.

Common Ego Defenses

The definition and function of self-image or ego defenses can be found in a number of behavioral science resource materials. Some of the more commonly used defenses will be discussed briefly.

Denial Of Reality

This defense is used to protect the self-image from unpleasant reality by refusing to perceive or face it. This form of escapist behavior is used to avoid facing or coping with a problem that threatens the self-image. Denial of reality is like the ostrich that supposedly buried its head in the sand to avoid facing a threatening situation.

Fantasizing

This is a way of gratifying frustrated or blocked desires in imaginary achievements. Sometimes fantasizing about what you can't have in reality may be emotionally healthy, but living in fantasy rather than recognizing the true situation can be damaging.

Compensation

An attempt to cover up self-image weakness by emphasizing desirable traits, or exaggerating ability or accomplishments is known as compensation. It may be used to compensate for frustration in one area by overgratification in another. Using substitute goals as a response to feelings of failure in not achieving original goals is a form of compensation. The pursuit of second-best goals as a way of life can lead to inferior feelings and weaken the self-image.

Projection

Projection results in placing the blame for personal difficulties or failures on others, or attributing one's own unethical desires to others. It is the tendency to accuse another person of one's own inadequacies or to look for scapegoats.

Rationalization

This is another defense mechanism that involves an attempt to prove that one's behavior is "rational" and justifiable, and thus worthy of self and social approval. In order to protect the self-image, people will consider only one motive or reason for their actions while denying all other possibilities. Failure to consider a number of different possible reasons for one's actions is a commonly used self-image defense. People with a negative self-image will rationalize their motives and actions, and will strongly resist any attempts to consider or explore other possibilities for them.

Repression

This is one of the most basic forms of defense, and consists of preventing painful or dangerous thoughts from entering consciousness. It results from being unwilling or unable to face threatening situations that seem likely to produce anxiety, fear or guilt. If one does not have the self-image strength to face a critical situation, it may be repressed into the unconscious. Repression is usually an involuntary or unconscious defense that can prevent one from facing or dealing with unpleasant life situations.

Reaction Formation

This is a defense that is used in an attempt to prevent uncomfortable or dangerous desires from being expressed. When one verbalizes exaggerated opposing attitudes or demonstrates completely opposite behavior intended as a barrier to revealing true beliefs or feelings, reaction formation is being used.

Displacement

This defense allows one to discharge pent-up feelings, usually of hostility or aggression, on objects less threatening or dangerous than those that initially aroused the emotion. This is used when people lack the self-image strength to confront the actual cause of their hostility or anger, and take it out on a less threatening person or object.

Emotional Insulation

In order to avoid emotional hurt or psychological pain, emotional insulation is used. This is done by withdrawing into passivity or indifference to protect the self from possible future hurt. It is, in effect, the cutting off of emotional feelings or responses to emotionally threatening human interactions.

Sympathism

This is another commonly used defense and results in one striving to gain sympathy from others in order to bolster feelings of self-worth despite personal failures.

Regression

As a defense mechanism regression involves the retreating to earlier developmental levels of childhood. This childlike behavior oftentimes stems from the inability to take responsibility or make decisions, and may include the lowering of aspirations. Those in the state of regression may have a strong desire to attach themselves to someone who will take care of them.

Intellectualizing

This refers to the defensive use of academic or technical language to express personal beliefs, attitudes and feelings. This defense mechanism is used to avoid personal or intimate disclosure, or authentic feelings and emotions. Intellectualizing is a means of depersonalizing relationships and maintaining safe or superficial distance from others, usually due to fear of rejection.

These are just some of the commonly used self-image defenses, and the reader is again reminded that it is the continuous overuse of these defenses that causes personal and human relation problems. If people have a positive self-image, they will have no need to overuse these defenses. Each time that a threatening situation is experienced, the person with a positive self-image will be able to realistically, without overuse of defenses, face that threat and respond to it in such a way that the self-image will be strengthened. When people respond defensively to threats to the self-image, they are actually placing a greater value on maintaining a negative self-image rather than on gaining positive self-image strength and personal growth.

These defense mechanisms are used as a crutch for a negative self-image. They are self-defenses that result in the loss of authenticity and real self-identity. They are facades used for the purpose of hiding feelings of inferiority or low self-esteem. Just as these defenses are artificial in their use, they are also illusionary in their protection. Not only are they intended to deceive others, but also they are self-deceptive because others can usually detect and see through them. Therefore, people who overuse these defenses in an attempt to gain acceptance will usually experience rejection because they will be seen as pretentious or phony. For people to drop the use of these self-image defenses, they must be accepted for what they are, not for what they pretend to be.

CHAPTER ELEVEN

You Are Your Most Valuable Possession

People with a negative self-image are prone to minimizing their self-worth. They seem to acquire the habit of telling how little they amount to and how insignificant they are in comparison to others. The habit of self-depreciation and self-devaluation can leave one bankrupt as a person. Nothing becomes more valuable to a person than total self-acceptance and an unqualified endorsement of self. Self-esteem requires that we continue to recognize our own uniqueness. We are the only one exactly like us in the world — with our own unique potentials, aptitudes, interests and natural inclinations.

Never Forfeit Appreciation Of Self And Sense Of Self-Worth

François Rabelais reminds us, *"So much is a man worth as he esteems himself."* It is essential for self-esteem that we never forfeit appreciation for ourselves and our sense of self-worth. To maintain our self-approval, we must continue to work to achieve our values and human potential. If we keep our self-approval, no matter what other objects of value we may lose, we will still be rich. We may make a fortune or we may lose one; we may live in a lavish beautiful home or in a modest dwelling; we may wear flashy expensive clothes or less pretentious attire; we can drive the finest new automobile or an old clunker; but regardless of our economic status in life, we have little of value if we don't value ourselves.

39

The following verse adeptly describes the price we must pay if we compromise our values or choose to barter with our self-approval:

Man In The Glass

When you get what you want in your struggle for wealth
*   And the world makes you king for a day,*
Just go to the mirror and look at yourself
*   And see what that man has to say.*

For it isn't your father or mother or wife
*   Upon whose judgment you pass,*
The fellow whose verdict counts most in your life
*   Is the one staring back from the glass.*

Some people may think you're a straight-shootin' chum
*   And call you a wonderful guy,*
But the man in the glass says you're only a bum
*   If you can't look him straight in the eye.*

He's the fellow to please, never mind all the rest
*   For he's with you clear to the end,*
And you've passed your most dangerous, difficult test
*   If the man in the glass is your friend.*

You may fool the whole world down the pathway of years
*   And get pats on the back as you pass,*
But your final reward will be heartaches and tears
*   If you've cheated the man in the glass.*

Anonymous

CHAPTER TWELVE

Self-Image And Human Relations

Not only is self-image a product of human relations and socialization, but also it has a profound effect on how we relate and get along or not get along, as the case may be, with others.

Generalizations About NSI And PSI People

Though it is true that no one has a totally positive or totally negative self-image, there are some generalizations that can be made about what could be called a negative self-image (NSI) or positive self-image (PSI) person. Some of these general distinctions will be made, and then how these personality traits or characteristics affect human relations and social interaction will be shown. Based on what has already been said about self-image, some possibilities may become quickly apparent to the reader. Some of these characteristics identified with either a NSI or a PSI person are based on my own subjective evaluation, but many of them have been more objectively determined by the results of standardized self-image tests or inventories that I have given to numerous counseling clients over the last 15 years.

First of all, it should be noted that individuals see everything in this world through the filter of their own self-image. Our self-image acts as a camera lens that can influence our perceptions, or the way we see things. As in using a camera, our lens may be out of focus. Selective perceptions can result from seeing what we choose or want to see. This, of course, can sometimes lead to a distortion of reality. If I think that you do not like me, I will tend to be especially attentive to anything you say or do that supports my belief, even though your dislike for me has never been truly verified. You may, in fact, like me very much, but my self-image lens or filter has caused a misinterpretation of your actions or communication toward me. This example sheds some light on why we are sometimes misunderstood in our communications and relationships with others.

Traits Of PSI And NSI People
That Influence Human Relations

Some of the general traits or characteristics between PSI and NSI people that can have a bearing or influence on human relations follow. People with PSI tend to radiate mental sunshine and cheerfulness. People with NSI have a diminished capacity to develop a friendly spirit and healthy sense of humor. In contrast PSI people can develop a good sense of humor — they can laugh at themselves, which is emotionally and mentally healthy. Often loaded down with personal problems, NSI people give the impression that the whole world rests on their shoulders. But PSI people are able to cope with problems in living and fulfill their needs. They are not only the most joyous and the happiest, but also the most friendly and sociable. People with PSI tend to look on the bright side of life. On the other hand, NSI people have little fun in life and are prone to living a boring humdrum existence. With optimism about the future, PSI people see success ahead; with pessimism about the future, NSI people see only failure.

In addition, PSI people are magnanimous and forgiving while NSI people are vindictive grudge collectors. Respecting the dignity and worth of others, PSI people tend to treat others well and form the habit of helping and encouraging them. Conversely, NSI people tend to diminish the dignity and respect of others, often putting them down to make themselves look better. While NSI people are overly sensitive to criticism, they may be excessively critical of others. They can be self-destructive, and in their own efforts to destroy themselves, they destroy others in the process. Usually socially distant, NSI people have rendered themselves incapable of being happy and cheerful, and thus deprive themselves of experiencing joy and fulfillment in life. One cannot long sustain good feelings and cheerfulness when in their company. Their negative and pessimistic attitude takes the fun and excitement out of life.

Some of the distinguishing characteristics between PSI and NSI people can clearly have an impact on social relationships. PSI people are a joy to be with. They see the good in others and find people as being kind and accommodating. With just the opposite attitude toward life and others, NSI people tend to fret and complain, always finding fault with everything and everyone. They see no cause for joy and look on the world as a cold, dismal, forbidding place — and they tend to find just what they are looking for.

Human relations tend not to be static — they either grow or they die. There is an old saying in psychology: "Neurosis seeks its own level." In other words, NSI people tend to seek out other NSI people to validate and reinforce their negative feelings toward self. Of course, the same process applies to PSI people. When two PSI people get together, such as in a marital relationship, they seem to say, "I'm okay, you're okay, and together we're better." They bring out the best in each other and encourage each other's growth. Liking themselves, they are not defensive or possessive. They form interdependent and cooperative relationships. They work to fulfill their potential as a couple while encouraging individual potential development in each other.

Two NSI people forming an intimate relationship, such as marriage, tend to bring out the worst in each other. It is as if they say, "I'm not okay, you're not okay, and together we're worse." They form competitive rather than cooperative relationships. They may become extremely dependent on and possessive of each other, becoming insecure, mistrustful and jealous. This can lead to a toxic relationship ending in emotional or physical abuse or both. A frequent NSI-plus-NSI marital relationship is that of the drinking couple. It is quite interesting to note that if an alcoholic relationship ends in divorce, one or both parties will invariably end up being attracted to another alcoholic.

The impact of self-image on human relationships is almost limitless but hopefully enough has been said here to impress the reader about the significance of self-image and self-esteem in our everyday contacts with other people. One with a positive self-image and self-esteem obviously has a comparative advantage in forming friendly, caring and loving relationships with others.

In summary, our own image of self determines the quality of relationships that we are capable of establishing with our fellow human beings.

CHAPTER THIRTEEN

Self-Image In
The World Of Work

For most of us, our occupation or profession is closely tied to our self-image. When meeting a new acquaintance, introductory comments will usually include information about people's occupation or area of work as part of their personal identity. Having a job that is fulfilling and rewarding, and that promotes challenge and growth can enhance self-esteem. To be stuck in a boring, mundane, uninteresting job can be a constant source of frustration, irritation and unhappiness. Working below one's potential or having no opportunity for future advancement can stifle human growth and self-actualization.

It is most important that people be aware of their potentials and limitations. Knowing one's aptitudes, interests, values and natural inclinations can help one to find the right job that will increase the chances for job satisfaction and self-esteem. When seeking employment, we need to evaluate our personal values, goals, talents, skills and former achievements.

To be working in an occupation that holds the promise of providing self-fulfillment and personal satisfaction can provide the motivation for achieving human potential and growth. The opportunity of achieving occupational goals helps people to feel good about themselves. As stated earlier, self-esteem is the product of self-actualization and human growth. A job that does not assist people in achieving their potential can be a disdainful and disparaging experience resulting in self-dislike, self-rejection and self-contempt. Working in an unfulfilling and unrewarding job can have a negative impact on self-confidence, self-respect and self-esteem.

A positive self-image is built on accomplishment or fulfillment of matching the truth about our own potentials and limitations. Without a sense of accomplishment and personal achievement, genuine self-confidence and authentic self-esteem are impossible to achieve.

One of the goals of work should be to help workers to become more self-actualizing and to realize their own potentials. Maslow's theory of self-actualization has been frequently adopted in business and employee relations studies. It has been found that employees need more than just a paycheck to be happy. It is clear that money is no longer the sole determinant of job satisfaction. Employees must also have the opportunity of fulfilling self-actualization and self-esteem needs. Studies show that most workers do not strike just for more money. Employee grievances and complaints are more often related to working conditions that deprive workers of dignity, self-respect and personal growth. It is well known that the treatment of workers on the job has a strong bearing on the work performance and output.

Job Stress

Experience as a vocational education counselor and as employee relations instructor has helped me gain insight and knowledge about factors contributing to workers' self-realization and self-esteem needs. When workers do not achieve these needs, job stress is likely to occur. Signs of job stress include fatigue, lack of enthusiasm for work and job burnout. Job burnout can happen to anyone who does not experience job satisfaction and fulfillment in the workplace. Job-related stress costs our society millions of dollars per year in decreased productivity, absenteeism and employee-relation problems. (More on self-image and stress management can be found in Chapter 14.)

The Right Job — A Positive Factor

Lack of job fulfillment results in emotional exhaustion, feelings of failure, and above all, decreased feelings of self-worth and self-esteem. It is most important, therefore, that we be in an occupation that holds the promise of achieving some degree of self-fulfillment and personal gratification commensurate with our potentials, values, aptitudes, interests and aspirations. We like the work that we are best suited to, and to not have this kind of work can result in boredom and lack of purpose.

We cannot always change our work circumstances, but we can change our reactions and responses to these situations. Workers with a PSI are able to maintain a high degree of positive self-control and are more likely to find joy and satisfaction in their work. They are secure in themselves and have a sense of self-confidence and self-reliance. Having the right job can be a very positive factor in our personal search for self-esteem.

CHAPTER FOURTEEN

Self-Image And Stress Management

Stress is often the result of a dynamic and changing society. Each of us is affected by the need to respond and adapt to a rapidly changing world. Alvin Toffler in his best-selling book *Future Shock* refers to our modern age as "the age of anxiety." He describes the increasing pace of our society and the stress that comes with this rapid change. Toffler makes it clear that there are serious emotional and physical costs for those who are unable to cope with stresses of the modern-day world. Each one of us undergoes stress in our daily living. Avoiding stress is not possible because almost everything we do has the potential of creating some degree of stress.

Two Types Of Stress

Dr. Hans Selye, one of the most well-known researchers of stress, defines stress as "the response of the body to any demand put upon it." He identifies two types of stress: **distress**, which is seen as negative stress, and **eustress**, which is defined as positive stress. This positive, or eustress, keeps us alert, challenged and stimulated. Distress, on the other hand, can be both physically and mentally damaging. Selye believes that negative stress results in ulcers, heart attacks, high blood pressure and strokes. Stress is something that most of us try to avoid; but according to Selye, eustress can actually be good for us because without it, we'd lack the energy, enthusiasm and motivation to act or respond to life's demands and challenges. While some stress is good, Selye is quick to caution that too much stress, or distress, can be dangerous to both our physical and mental well-being.

Stress is an inevitable part of life. Studies are now showing a direct relationship between self-image and stress. How we think and feel about ourselves (self-image) directly influences the way we react or respond to life stressors. Research also shows that not just the negative events in our lives, such as loss of a job, can cause stress; the positive circumstances as well, such as getting a job promotion, can produce stress. Not only the large happenings in life result in stress, but also the continuous series of small events tend to build up over time, providing fuel for a negative stress reaction.

Two major functions of the self-image are to assist one in coming to grips with inevitable life problems, and to fulfill both physical and social needs. As NSI people experience failure in coping with life's problems and satisfying needs, they may experience strong feelings of distress. Most of the distress comes from the perceptions, meanings and interpretations given to the situations and circumstances producing the distress. The manner in which individuals will define or interpret a stressful experience is very much related to their self-image. Adopting the right temperament and attitude toward self can have a profound effect on stress management.

Positive Self-Esteem Helps Stress Management

As stated earlier, self-esteem is the value and worth that you attribute to yourself. When we acquire a good sense of self-acceptance, self-confidence, self-trust, self-reliance and self-esteem, we clearly have a comparative advantage in successfully managing stress. To maintain a positive self-image and self-esteem, we must continue to appreciate ourselves as valuable and worthwhile individuals. We must focus on our positive traits and human potentials. All of us have unique talents, abilities, interests, aptitudes and potentials that we can use and develop more fully. We must be willing to own these assets and strong points if we wish to experience personal growth and positive change. It is essential that we continue to develop a positive self-image and self-esteem if we are to successfully meet the challenges and stresses of modern-day life.

There are currently a number of excellent books available dealing with stress and stress management that will augment this short chapter on the subject. Nevertheless, it is important to remember that all people experience stress, and it is up to them to individually determine their own stress levels. As we continue the journey in the search for self-esteem, we will gain a greater ability to constructively use positive stress while reducing the negative stress in our life.

CHAPTER FIFTEEN

Becoming A Self-Image Builder To Others

In the process of conducting **Self-Image Modification Training** workshops around the country, I am frequently asked the following kinds of questions:

1. How can I become a positive self-image builder to others?
2. What are some of the things I must know and do to help others with self-esteem enhancement?
3. How can I be a more positive influence in the self-esteem development of my child, my spouse, my co-worker or my friend?

A brief summation of the ways in which NSI people think and feel about themselves can provide insights on establishing a "helping" relationship. People with NSI harbor personal feelings of worthlessness. They tend to see themselves as life failures and to believe they lack the ability to change. They are generally unhappy, unfulfilled, anxious and lonely individuals who have lost trust in themselves and their ability to establish trusting relationships with others. They feel a sense of hopelessness, helplessness and discouragement. They are highly defensive and have trouble fulfilling needs and managing their lives.

Special Skills, Talents And Attributes

Considering all of these characteristics of NSI people, what special skills, talents and attributes do we have to have in order to help them to feel better about themselves and to become more responsible for changing themselves and their own lives for the better?

49

Knowledge And Sensitivity

First of all, there are no simple answers to this question. It is essential, however, that we be knowledgeable and sensitive to the causal factors of low self-esteem and that we avoid becoming judgmental or moralistic about this problem. Remember that self-image is basically a product of socialization and learning, and that NSI is not in any way indicative of a disgraceful condition, moral impairment or character deficiency. In addition, maintain the "assumption of worth" attitude toward others. Believe that all people are "born gifted" in their own way and that they have the innate potential to experience positive growth and change. Remain confident about those we are trying to help so that we can truly assist them in the search for a new identity and self-esteem. Having a personal philosophy of "humanistic equality" toward all human beings is a prerequisite for building self-image in others. One who holds attitudes of bigotry, prejudice and discrimination toward others cannot enhance self-esteem in others or in themselves. Nothing has been a greater obstruction in the development of a positive self-image and self-esteem in countless numbers of people in our society than racial prejudice and discrimination.

Positive Image Of Self

To effectively build self-image in others, we must have a reasonably positive image of ourselves. We must be a PSI role model. This requires that we demonstrate the personal traits and characteristics of a PSI person. This then requires that we must be accepting of ourselves as adequate, capable and worthwhile individuals. We cannot project the image of one who "has arrived," but one who is in the "process of becoming." We must be fulfilling our needs in a responsible manner and managing our problems in living. An NSI person attempting to help another with low self-esteem to become more self-reliant would be something like the "blind leading the blind."

To be an effective "helping person" to others, it is essential that we establish a relationship of complete acceptance of the other person. This relationship is what the well-known client-centered therapist, Dr. Carl Rogers, referred to as "unconditional positive regard." This does not mean we must condone what others may be doing or accept their values for ourselves. It simply means that there needs to be a relationship of unconditional acceptance of the dignity and worth of the other person. This relationship must be built on a foundation of mutual acceptance, trust and respect.

Empathy

Empathy is another important ingredient of a "helping" relationship. Empathy refers to the capacity for people to put themselves in the other person's place. Though total empathy probably cannot be completely experienced, we must be willing to "walk in the other person's shoes." This requires the ability and willingness to hear what other people are saying and to feel what they are feeling. This requires sensitive, careful and effective listening. Having an accurate and nonjudgmental understanding of what the other person is saying and feeling is essential if we are to realize our potential as effective builders of self-image in others.

Encouragement

One of the most important roles that we can play in a "helping-person" relationship to others is that of an encourager. Encouragement is necessary in assisting another to grow and change. Often fearful of change, NSI people avoid taking the necessary risks that positive change requires. As stated earlier, it is common for NSI people to sabotage their efforts in the self-image building process.

To be effective encouragers, we must make NSI people believe that we are genuinely interested in their progress and growth. We, as helpers, must reflect the sincere attitude of caring concern and encouragement. Encouragement is such an important part of the "helping-person" process that it will be covered in more detail in the next chapter.

CHAPTER SIXTEEN

The Need For Encouragement And Support

We all need encouragement and support in the human growth process. Psychologists tend to agree that we all require at least one "significant other" in our lives with whom we can share our innermost thoughts, feelings and concerns. We also need others with whom we can form meaningful and trusting relationships — caring friends who can be respected and whose opinions can be relied on. In their book *Shifting Gears* Nena and George O'Neill refer to this kind of intimate relationship as "feedback friends":

> When we are in crisis or need to make changes and decisions in our life, these are the kinds of friends we need the most. In our discussions with them, we gain some objectivity about our problems and selves. These friends may share with us their troubles, similar problems and the mistakes and successes they may have made. Knowing that we are not alone in our struggles, suffering and mistakes and that others share the imperfections of man's existence can give us solace and a feeling of commonality and the inspiration to go on.

Group Process

Having had considerable training and many years of experience in social group work, I feel strongly that support groups can be most effective as a "helping person" resource if properly facilitated. Group process is not on trial.

53

One only has to look in any city or community local paper under the heading Self-Help Groups to see how popular these human resources have become. Groups such as Alcoholics Anonymous, Narcotics Anonymous, Al-Anon and Alateen, Adult Children of Alcoholics, Overeaters Anonymous, Co-dependents Anonymous, Parents Anonymous and Gamblers Anonymous, just to name a few, are available all hours of the day or night and easily accessible to anyone who needs them.

Successes

Group process is a peer counseling or training technique that has been successful in assisting participants to better understand themselves and gain insight about others. Groups can provide assistance, recognition, encourage-ment and support to those who are in the process of human growth and change. Self-help groups are voluntary small group structures capable of providing "helping" relationships that we all must have to fulfill our social needs. These groups are usually formed by peers who have come together for mutual assistance and support. Self-help groups provide a human source for interpersonal learning. Tending to promote personal and social responsibility among the members, these groups may also provide a philosophy or value system through which members can attain an enhanced sense of personal identity and self-esteem.

Problems

As committed as I am to the use of group process, I do have a few personal reservations about questionable approaches that are sometimes used. Having clocked a number of hours in so-called encounter or sensitivity groups, I am aware of some who have experienced psychic wounds from these experiences although I personally did not. This damage is usually because of the lack of skill or training by the group facilitator. Any "clod" can open wounds, but it can take considerable talent, knowledge and expertise to heal them.

Another problem with some groups is the over-emphasis on "insight therapy." Some groups spend considerable time on facilitating self-awareness but do not provide for the translation of this awareness to action. Personal stories tend to get told over and over again, but nothing is ever done or accomplished to solve the problem. Some people tire of hearing repetitious testimonials while seeing nothing else happening. Of course, there are always a few members, for neurotic reasons of their own, who seem to enjoy telling "one-upmanship" or "can you top this" stories. I shall not make value judgments as to what these people contribute or fail to contribute to the group, but I tend to be suspicious of people who have this need to call attention to themselves.

Group process implies growth or change, and if the group does not move forward from the awareness to the action, i.e., "what to do about the problem" stage, members can lose interest. This experience can lead to further frustration, and feelings of hopelessness can increase. In short, group members must feel they are getting something from the group if they are to truly benefit from the group's potential to facilitate human growth.

Powerful Human Resource

Groups can generate a powerful human resource for positive growth and change. The identity of individuals is derived from the meaningfulness of their relationships with others. Self-identity or "who and what we are" is established through our identification with individuals and groups that are significant and meaningful to us. Because self-image is acquired through group interaction, it is logical that self-image can be changed through group participation. Social interaction provides for inner awareness and self-esteem. The group can also function as a viable resource of encouragement and support for those who are striving to better achieve their potential and human growth.

Other Sources For Encouragement And Support

Encouragement and support are not unique to group activity. Everywhere we go, we find opportunities to give support and encouragement to others. Everywhere we see someone who needs encouragement and understanding — someone who needs a lift. For many people, a kind gesture or word has been a turning point in enhancing self-esteem. There are many people in our society who may be on the edge of despair with no one to turn to for help. How many suicides could be prevented if more people were available to give encouragement and support to others in time of desperate need?

Cultivation Of The Great Natural High

As I've indicated, self-esteem needs to be enhanced and developed. Self-esteem is the great medicine of the human spirit — the great natural high. The cultivation of self-esteem can transform our lives so that we can begin to see things in a more positive light. People with PSI and self-esteem are not only the happiest, but also the most productive and most successful. People with good self-esteem tend to look on the bright side of life, and are not likely candidates for depression or despondency. They do not live lives of a boring humdrum existence. People with NSI tend to be irritable, unhappy and disagreeable. They are continual faultfinders, always complaining and responding to others with rudeness or cutting sarcasm. They are incapable of radiating joy or happiness, or of showing caring concern for others or themselves.

People with low self-esteem build walls around themselves and then complain because they are not free. They become prisoners of their own making and the stones they use for their isolating walls are self-criticism, self-doubt and self-rejection. These are the people who can benefit most from encouragement and support.

Further information on the SIM Training group support system as a means of self-esteem enhancement can be found in SIM II, Chapter Twenty-Two, *Self-Image And Group Process*.

CHAPTER SEVENTEEN

Self-Reliance Versus Dependency

One of the questions that we, as human beings, frequently face is the question of self-reliance versus dependency. As human beings, we have many needs that must be satisfied if we are to live and grow in our physical and social environment. Some of these needs must be met by others while we must also develop the capacity to meet our own needs. In dealing with this conflict, it is easy to err by going too far in either direction.

For instance, as parents, we are counseled to maintain control over our small children while also giving them responsibility to make their own decisions in life. It is well-known that the normal growth and development of children can be stifled and retarded by overprotection, whereas children will usually experience frustration and failure if too much is expected of them too soon.

The question seems to be, "Could people do more to meet their own needs if they only would, or would they do more if they only could?" It is known that the image of self in terms of self-confidence, self-reliance, self-trust and self-control is directly related to how people fulfill their needs and deal with problems in living.

Individuals with NSI tend to feel insecure and inadequate. They tend to believe they are not responsible for what happens to them in this world and see themselves as being controlled by external forces. On the other hand, PSI people believe in the concepts of free will and free choice. They believe that as human beings we are creatures of choice, and that we can take full responsibility for our own thinking, feelings and behavior.

Locus of control studies indicate that PSI people tend to live lives of preferences and choices while those with NSI are more susceptible to living lives of indecision and dependencies. People with PSI internalize success and externalize failure. They tend to own their success and take credit for their achievements, and do not overreact to their failures. In contrast, NSI people are more likely to internalize failure and externalize success. They take full responsibility for their failures in life but see their successes as an act of fate or just plain good luck. They acquire an image of "failure identity," and lack the qualities of self-efficacy and self-control.

Understanding The Dilemma

To better understand the dilemma between dependency and independence, it is probably best to recognize that both of these terms realistically apply to all human beings. At birth we were totally dependent on adults for our mainte-nance and survival needs. As infants, we tended to respond at the dependency level for the fulfillment of our needs. Most life objectives were oriented toward avoiding pain and seeking pleasure.

The testing of reality was closely tied to reward and punishment, or as psychologists prefer to call it, the stimulus-response factor. As children, we were dependent on adults for our basic need fulfillment and overall well-being. As we grew to adulthood, some of our dependencies continue to exist. It is well-known that the human being does not do well when exposed to physical and emotional isolation. The failure-to-thrive syndrome studies of infants clearly show that when the infant is deprived of social and physical contact with a significant other (preferably the natural mother), bonding does not take place, and the infant's ability to experience normal healthy adjustment and develop-ment is jeopardized.

As we grow to adulthood, we continue to be dependent on others in order to fulfill our social needs of recognition, belonging, acceptance and affection. Of course, we also remain dependent on others for the exchange of economic material goods and services.

The problem of looking at dependency versus independence is to see this as an either-or issue. Many people see any degree of dependency as bad and have the false notion that healthy people are those who can function totally alone and fulfill all their needs by themselves. Of course, this is an impossible task and can become as much of a problem as the other extreme of accepting no responsibility for ourselves.

Overdependency

Keeping dependency in its proper perspective, we'll now deal with what might be called excessive or overdependency. Overdependent people function by not having a positive identity. They do not have a good sense of self regarding potentials and limitations, or of personal values underlying life goals and objectives. To experience success and self-fulfillment in our world, it is necessary to acquire a positive image of self and internalized self-control. People with PSI believe in themselves, and see themselves as capable and self-reliant individuals who can cope with problems in living and can fulfill needs. Conversely, NSI people tend to believe they are victims in life. Dependency is a condition that deprives dependent people of their freedom to choose their own course of action in life. To be overly dependent means to give up one's freedom of choice and self-control. Through the acquisition of a more positive self-image and self-esteem, one can eliminate neurotic or parasitic dependencies that can stifle positive self-confidence and self-reliance.

Normal Or Healthy Interdependence

In our complex and ever-changing society, we should not lose sight of the fact that as social beings "no man is an island" and that all human beings remain dependent on others to some degree. This dependency may be thought of as normal or healthy interdependence. We must not confuse "healthy" human interdependency with neurotic "sick" dependency, which can rob us of our potential to experience human growth and the good feelings that come with influencing and controlling our present and future lives. A thought worth remembering is, *"No one can let us down unless we are leaning on them."* It is important that we maintain a realistic balance between self-reliance and dependency as a means of self-esteem enhancement.

Another dependency source is the reliance on mood-altering chemicals that has become such a common experience in our society. Chapter 18 is devoted to this specialized dependency, and its relationship to self-image and self-esteem.

CHAPTER EIGHTEEN

Self-Image And Chemical Dependency

Chemical dependency has been identified as a leading national social, economic and health problem. Over a decade of work in the chemical dependency field and a comprehensive review of the substance abuse literature have convinced me that a common core underlying substance abuse activity is NSI. Whether this NSI is a causal factor or result of chemical dependency may be debatable, but its existence remains reasonably conclusive.

Life's Most Critical Factor — Lack Of Self-Esteem

Lilburn S. Barksdale has devoted many years to the study of self-image and self-esteem, and makes the following statement:

Lack of self-esteem is truly the most critical factor in everyone's life, for practically all our problems stem either directly or indirectly from crippling or low self-esteem. For example, alcoholism and other drug addictions are usually the result of an effort to escape the self and individual hates or dislikes, to avoid the misery or emotional hurting engendered by self-rejection.

Understanding The True Nature Of Substance Abuse

According to the *American Medical Association Manual On Alcoholism* (1977), it is generally accepted that alcoholism stems not from a single cause,

61

but from a complicated interplay of **physiological, psychological** and **sociological** factors. This holistic health approach to the explanation of substance abuse, which includes both the medical and social model theories of chemical dependency, would seem to make the most sense when attempting to understand the true nature of substance abuse activity.

In gaining insight about the substance abuse problem, it is a serious mistake to ignore that substance abuse results in a mood- or mind-altering experience. Those who abusively use psychoactive or mind-altering chemicals probably do so because of the sensation or mood-changing experience the drug creates for the user. The alcoholic, for instance, will continue to drink excessively in order to experience the feeling of intoxication. One does not have to hear many Alcoholics Anonymous testimonials to be convinced of this. Here, one will find frequent references to the use of alcohol as a means of coping with life's pain.

A common factor related to the use of psychoactive chemicals is that they can act to lessen users' feelings of emotional pain and their sense of inadequate well-being. Alcohol and other drug dependence is very often a characteristic of the way one is attempting to cope with problems in living. In trying to deal with life's problems, one may turn to alcohol, narcotics, barbiturates, tranquilizers and other mood-altering chemicals. Substance abuse is thus largely determined by drug users' thinking and feelings about self and how they are, or are not, managing life and fulfilling needs. When people believe or feel that they cannot cope with the real world, a retreat from reality may be sought through the use of alcohol and/or other psychoactive chemicals. Since these drugs tend to have a mind-altering effect, their excessive use may be seen as a means of seeking relief and comfort from unpleasant experiences or stressful situations. In other words, one will gravitate to drug use as a means of feeling better, or at least to avoid feeling worse. Drug dependence may result in an attempt to reduce negative feelings such as stress, tension, frustration, guilt and anxiety. However, it is well-known that the use of mind-altering chemicals will lessen drug users' abilities to deal effectively with their life stresses. When people lack the self-image strength to cope with problems in living, they may become involved in the self-destructive cycle of drug dependence. This cycle of drug dependence is seen as personally destructive because one's image of self becomes further diminished as chemical dependency increases.

The authors of the book, *Drugs and Alcohol* (3rd ed. 1979), write the following regarding self-esteem and drug dependency:

> Everyone needs self-esteem — a feeling of personal worth or value. The daily lives of a great many of us, perhaps most of us, are greatly influenced by our efforts to fulfill this need. Self-esteem is one of the hardest needs to satisfy in an alcoholic or other drug abuser. A "vicious cycle" may be set up in which lack of self-esteem motivates drug

dependency, while the drug dependency causes a further loss of self-esteem. Until something intervenes to break this cycle of hopelessness, drug abuse is likely to continue. For many people, the best way to start building self-esteem is to find some activity in which success is attainable. This could be in a job, a hobby, a sport or in service to others. Activities are especially helpful when they combine a sense of personal achievement with acceptability to other people.

Though there is no consensus regarding the causal factors related to **alcoholism**, one of our most serious social, economic and health problems, there is significant evidence that a relationship between self-image and alcohol abuse does exist. The noted psychiatrist, Dr. Abraham J. Twerski, in his book, *Like Yourself — And Others Will Too*, makes the following statement pertaining to self-image and alcoholism:

> There is a factor common to many alcoholics, and that is the negative self-image. In my own clinical experience, I have yet to see the exception. I have yet to see an alcoholic from any walk of life, from skid row to the most affluent, from uneducated to the highest levels of academic achievement, who does not suffer from a poor self-esteem that antedated the drinking.

Hope For Overcoming NSI And Low Self-Esteem

A negative image of self can be a serious handicap in living a happy, productive and harmonious life. There is hope, however, for those with NSI and low self-esteem because it is possible to undergo positive self-image changes if one is sincerely committed to doing so. If this were not true, those suffering from the symptoms of self-image problems, such as alcoholism and other drug dependencies, would be hopelessly entrapped within their self-destructive behavior pattern, and would have no hope for a better and more meaningful life.

CHAPTER NINETEEN

Self-Image And Wellness

Few people realize that many of their ailments can be emotionally induced. Our self-image has a lot to do with both our physical and mental well-being. When we allow ourselves to be governed by our emotions and moods, we can open the door to the enemies of our health, success and happiness. Some people actually attract illness to themselves by constantly thinking about it. We can fix images of sickness in our minds that can lower our resistance to illness and make the body more susceptible to the very thing we fear. There is some truth to the adage, *"If we think healthy thoughts, we attract health."*

Most doctors can recall patients who, on being told they have a serious illness, seem to give up and soon wither and die, while others who refuse to accept the diagnosis live out their lives with unexplained energy, suffering less pain and fewer physical symptoms.

As pointed out in holistic health, mind and body function together and neither one totally exists without the other.

The Greek philosopher Socrates expressed this idea when he said, *"There is no illness of the body apart from the mind."*

Research in psychosomatic illness indicates that there is no real scientific method to completely control the interaction of mind (psyche) and body (soma), but there is reasonably good evidence to suggest that a person's mental state can contribute to disease.

Studies are showing that people with PSI and self-esteem seem to enjoy more robust health, avoid debilitating disease, and deal more effectively with factors that can increase susceptibility to both physical and mental illness. As

65

indicated in the preceding section on chemical dependency, chemicals, such as alcohol and other mood-altering drugs, may provide temporary relief from the anxieties and stresses of life; but there are no chemical solutions to life's problems. We are living in a drug society, and though there are many wonder drugs available to both prevent and cure disease, many commonly used drugs, including tobacco, can contribute to poor health problems.

Maintenance Of Physical And Mental Well-Being

A healthy attitude and positive image of self can have a significant influence in maintaining both physical and mental well-being. It is well-known, for instance, that we are more susceptible to disease when under emotional stress. It has been found that a wide range of illnesses, such as high blood pressure, migraine headaches, ulcers, allergies, arthritis, heart disease and digestive disorders, are attributable to anxiety and stress reactions. Biofeedback machines that are designed to give audible or visual signals whenever physiological changes occur have helped us understand more about the relationship between mind and body. The use of these machines has demonstrated that patients can actually learn to control their bodies' processes mentally. Of course, much still needs to be learned about how mental factors actually affect physical health; but it would appear that having a positive self-image and self-confidence can provide significant self-protection not only against mental but also against physical ills. Building PSI and enhancing self-esteem may very well function as a kind of inexpensive health insurance.

CHAPTER TWENTY

Self-Image And Positive Self-Control

Many of us have been taught to believe that we are controlled by external circumstances and events — that we are regulated and dominated by forces outside ourselves. Many theories of human behavior tend to reduce the human being to a stimulus response machine or genetically programmed robot with little or no freedom and choice in life. Believing that our actions and behavior are caused by forces outside of us suggests that we are simply driven or controlled machines, not living, thinking human beings. Gordon Allport sheds light on the origin of many of our behavioral science theories when he writes:

> Some theories of human behavior are based largely upon the behavior of sick and anxious people or upon the antics of captive and desperate rats. Fewer theories have derived from the study of healthy human beings, those who strive not so much to preserve life as to make it worth living. Thus we find today many studies of criminals, few of law-abiders; many of fear, few of courage; more on hostility than on affiliation, much on the blindness in man, little on his vision, much on his past, little on his outreaching into the future.

Self-Image Affects Management Of Life

In the area of self-image research, it seems apparent that people's image of self has much to do with how they manage their life. People's image of self in terms of self-acceptance, self-reliance, self-confidence and self-control is directly related to how they fulfill their needs and deal with problems in living. People with PSI accept the premise that just about everything they think, feel and do comes from within and not from outside themselves. Individuals with NSI or low self-esteem tend to believe that they are not responsible for what happens to them in this world and see themselves as being controlled by unavoidable outside forces. On the other hand, PSI people believe in the concepts of free will and free choice, and take full responsibility for their own decisions and actions. In his program, "The Psychology of Winning," Dr. Denis Waitley states the following about positive self-control:

> Winners realize they personally have the power to take control of many more aspects of their lives, both mental and physical, than were heretofore thought possible. They know that barring organic damage or congenital faults, self-control is the key to both mental and physical health and can contribute enormously to total well-being . . . .

Those who have a positive image of self and internalized self-control actively seek to understand and control their surroundings and themselves. They are willing to take responsibility for their actions, accepting both the positive and negative consequences of their conduct, decisions and behavior. However, people with NSI function as though the locus of control is an externalized process. They tend to believe that fate, chance, powerful others, or complex environmental conditions determine what happens to them.

Positive self-control allows people to choose among life alternatives and to determine their own destinies. It is a true but sad commentary that our society is filled with people who have lost effective control of themselves and their lives. These people tend to rely on chance, fate, luck or even their astrological signs to determine what they believe to be their destinies in life. They live in a world of indecision and are afraid to make up their own minds for fear of making a mistake or having to accept the responsibility for a wrong choice. They are reluctant to take a stand on their values, and are unable to define and achieve personal life goals. They leave the achievement of their human potentials, abilities, talents and accomplishments to chance, thereby forfeiting the opportunity for personal growth and self-realization.

It is through personal effort and self-determination that we can build a strong and long-lasting foundation for a positive self-image and self-esteem. Maintaining PSI and self-esteem is the best insurance and protection that we can have from the loss of both physical and mental self-control. The loss of positive self-control can lead to serious damaging and self-destructive behavior. In their book *Winners and Losers*, Dr. Howard M. Newburger and Marjorie Lee write the following regarding the important role that PSI plays in maintaining both physical and psychological well-being:

Those with well-defined strong positive self-images don't tend to become drug addicts, alcoholics, psychotics, chronic depressives, or suicides. When specific external stress does bring about mental illness, the positive self-image people bounce back far more quickly.

Having PSI and self-esteem can provide us with the inner strength and self-determination to face life's challenges in an enthusiastic, optimistic and responsible manner. Those with NSI, however, will find the notion of self-responsibility and self-determination too threatening, and will be quick to abandon their potential for positive self-control. Positive self-image people accept themselves as creatures of choice and not just mindless instruments of external controlling forces. They know they alone have the power of positive self-control that allows them the opportunity of fulfilling their own life values and goals.

The Power Within

We each have the power within us to choose happiness over unhappiness, self-fulfillment over self-defeat and hope over despair. We are not pushed forward by mysterious or unconscious motivating forces from the past, but instead are pulled ahead by our self-determined hopes, plans and intentions for the future. Individuals with PSI function on a rational and self-motivating level, fully aware of the forces that guide them, and are also able to have positive self-control over those forces.

The need for contemporary and future meaning, purpose and hope in our lives is most essential for personal growth and self-realization, which will be discussed in the following chapter.

CHAPTER TWENTY-ONE

The Need For Meaning, Purpose And Hope

We make the world we live in and, to a large degree, shape our own environment. We are not just victims of our environment but rather interpreters of our physical and social surroundings. We are responsible for choosing the person we are today and are, therefore, responsible for choosing the person we wish to become tomorrow. People with PSI and self-esteem tend to be optimistic about the future. Those with feelings of insecurity, vulnerability and self-doubt tend to view the future with anxiety and trepidation while those with a greater sense of self-confidence and self-reliance see the future as an opportunity for personal challenge and growth.

We Can Influence Our Future

Though no one can be sure what the future holds, it is still possible to influence many outcomes. People who lack a sense of positive self-reliance and self-direction tend to believe that their choices and actions have little or no influence on life events, and that nothing one does or can do will make any difference about present or future happenings. One may acquire a kind of "learned helplessness," which implies that one is merely a victim of chance, circumstance or fate. In contrast, people with more PSI and self-reliance generally believe that they can exert a high level of influence and control over their present and future lives. They believe that they are, to a large degree, masters of their own fate and that they can learn from the past, live for today, and most importantly, plan for the future.

Bruno Bettelheim gives us insight about our need for hope, meaning and purpose in our future in the following:

If we hope to live not just from moment to moment, but in true consciousness of our existence, then our greatest need and most difficult achievement is to find meaning, purpose and hope in our lives.

It is most satisfying and fulfilling to go through life spreading hope instead of despair, encouragement instead of discouragement and love instead of hate. The more we give of ourselves, the more we can grow as a person. Hopelessness is the enemy of human growth and aliveness. Hope can make the difference between simply existing or living. Some people live in the gloomy dungeons of their own making and then complain of the darkness, while others prefer to live in the light of meaning, purpose and hope for their present and future lives.

Growth Requires Willingness

Growth requires the willingness to take risks in the search for self-esteem. We must continue to have faith and hope in our ability to change and grow as a person. We must have hope for the future in order to have the courage to set new life goals leading to the enhancement of a more positive identity and self-esteem. Personal growth and self-realization mean that our attitudes, needs, values and goals all change with age, new experiences and increased self-knowledge. People's image of self can be continually modified to match their new standards, beliefs, goals, personal expectations and achievements. As people acquire genuine appreciation and regard for their own human dignity and worth as a person, they will find increasing hope for a fuller and better world. Perhaps this point is best expressed in the words of Dr. Karl Menninger, *"Where there is life, there is hope; but also, where there is hope there is life."*

Obviously, it is impossible to go through life without some negative experiences — experiences that create self-doubt, and put questions in our minds about our own abilities and sense of self-worth. These kinds of life circumstances contribute to a NSI and low self-esteem. On the other hand, a more positive image of self can be achieved through the accumulation of successful and rewarding experiences. People with PSI see life as a journey rather than a destination. They view life adjustments and changes as challenges to be met rather than obstacles to be overcome. A positive view of self provides the basis for great personal strength. In contrast, people with NSI tend to hold a low estimate of their abilities and potentials. Those who do not possess PSI see themselves as unliked, unwanted, unworthy, unimportant and unable to take on new life challenges with a sense of self-confidence, self-reliance and self-trust. This fear and feeling of insecurity render them unwilling to take the necessary risks needed to experience self-growth and personal change. They become defensive and often "freeze in the clutch" because of excessive fears and anticipatory anxiety. When fearful people withdraw within their defensive shell, communication with others is often blocked. This self-image defensiveness leads to losing touch with others who can be a supportive resource for encouragement, reassurance and understanding. As a result, those with NSI and low self-esteem develop an increased negative self-perception.

Self-Image Is Subject To Change

Our self-image is not static or fixed, and is always subject to change. As people work to acquire a more positive self-image and self-esteem, they can effectively (1) assess unique potentials and limitations, (2) clarify values and establish new value-goal relationships, (3) cope with problems in living, and (4) continue to grow as people. Arthur Combs provides an excellent summary of the functions of PSI when he writes:

> Having a positive view of self is much like having money in the bank. It provides the kind of security that permits the owner a freedom he could not have otherwise. With a positive view of self one can risk taking chances; one does not have to be afraid of what is new and different. A sturdy ship can venture further from port. Just so, an adequate person can launch himself without fear into the new, the untried and the unknown.

In our dynamic and ever-changing world, we are constantly faced with the need for the enhancement of self-esteem. The next part of this training manual, SIM II, provides a systematic growth-group experience facilitating the building of a more positive self-image and self-esteem. This growth support group program is designed to help participants assess their current self-image, explore their values and goals, and foster further progress in human growth and development.

PART TWO

SIM II — Self-Image Modification Training

*A systems approach to self-actualization
and human growth through
training-group participation*

INTRODUCTION — SIM II

The primary purpose of the first part of this training manual, SIM I, has been to acquaint you with a working knowledge of self-image theory and to provide information regarding the role that self-image and self-esteem play in everyday life. The purpose of SIM II is to provide you with the opportunity of applying self-image theory in your own life through participation in a training-group system approach to human growth and self-realization.

SIM Training utilizes a system framework designed to actualize human potential and build self-esteem. The system model emphasizes basic principles of organization and looks at all human beings in terms of systematic growth and development. A premise of SIM Training is that all individuals have one central need in life, which is to achieve their human potentialities. The human being is both an organic and functional system with the potential for human growth and change. All people have a need to work toward achieving their potential, to realize their values and to attain personal life goals.

The SIM Training system is designed for an eight-week group process regimen, with each session lasting one and one-half hour. (Group facilitators may wish to modify these suggested time boundaries in keeping with their special group needs.) A self-image inventory, group exercises and group participant tracking forms for the first four system functions are provided as a means of evaluating and measuring program achievements and outcomes.

Because each system function is designed to build on the next, it is important that each group member make a sincere commitment to attend each scheduled group session. This commitment is necessary in order to provide an effective support-group culture and to guarantee that group members receive the greatest benefit from their time spent in the sessions.

A unique characteristic of SIM Training is its application of several well-established human growth approaches including self-actualization, systems theory and group process. Each of these approaches is action or result oriented, and the synthesis of these combined techniques provides a synergistic and holistic process for human growth and change.

CHAPTER TWENTY-TWO

Self-Image And Group Process

Group process is a training technique that has been successful in assisting participants to better understand themselves and gain insight about others. Insight and awareness of self may be difficult to acquire alone, and it is through interaction with others that this can be best experienced and achieved. In the process of self-image change, self-awareness by itself is usually not enough. One must take action on this personal awareness if lasting change is to be realized. This action can be most productive through the process of planning and goal setting. Planning involves some degree of uncertainty and probability because we may not have complete control over all future events and circumstances. Having the belief, however, that we can determine and control many future life events is central to the SIM Training process.

Major Emphasis — Interaction Of Group Members

The major emphasis of group process in SIM Training will be on directly experiencing the kind of group that is suggested by Dr. Carl Rogers when he writes:

It usually consists of 10 to 15 persons and a facilitator or leader. Emphasis is upon the interactions among the group members, in an atmosphere which encourages each to drop his/her defenses and facades and thus enables the person to recognize and change self-defeating attitudes, test out and adopt more innovative and constructive behavior and subsequently to relate more adequately and effectively to others in everyday life . . .

Social groups, starting with the family, form the building blocks of the self-image. Fundamentally, self-image is developed by way of the feedback or reaction others give to the behavior of the self in social interaction. Self-identity or "who and what we are" is established through our identification with individuals and groups that are significant and meaningful to us. Social interaction in groups provides the potentials for inner awareness, self-image modification and personal growth.

Social Responsibility

As participants begin to become involved through group interaction, each member is encouraged to accept a sense of social responsibility for one another. Through demonstrating social responsibility, group members release their potential as "helping persons" both to themselves and to others. Social responsibility provides the means for responsible involvement with others, which is necessary in the maintenance of a positive self-image and a successful identity.

Constructive Feedback

One of the most valuable group experiences for the strengthening of self-image is constructive feedback. Feedback is a way of helping others to consider changing their concept of self and behavior. Communication with a person or a group of people gives people information about themselves and their effect on others in real-life human relationships. The group serves as a resource for congruent social responses and constructive feedback that are necessary for an individual to obtain authentic self-awareness and a positive identity. One's self-image is a product of feedback from others, and may be subject to distorted or faulty perceptions. Group feedback can serve as a collective resource for more accurate self-appraisals and validation.

Johari Window

In his book entitled *Group Processes* Dr. Joseph Luft describes a method for looking at group dynamics and the relations between self and others as a means for better understanding what happens in our relationships with others and for learning more about ourselves. The model, which depicts the way self-image is formed and modified, is called the **Johari Window** and is briefly illustrated in Figure 1.

When we meet other people, we bring with ourselves information or data that are known to us. We also have effects on other people that are known to us. People we meet have some data about us that are known to them, but there is a lot of information that they do not know about us. Also there are

	Known to Self	Not Known to Self
Known to Others	**A** Open Shared Area	**C** Blind Area
Not Known to Others	**B** Private Secret Area	**D** Unknown Undiscovered Area

**Figure 1. Johari Window — Model for Formation
and Modification of Self-Image**

some details that neither we nor others know about us. Some examples are why we become angry at certain times, why we are interested in some activities more than others or why our moods change. Thus, in **Box A** are the data of our public selves, known to us and known to others. On first meeting with other people, these data consist mainly of readily observable character- istics such as sex, size, color, etc.

In **Box B** are data known to us but not known to others. These might include details about our background, family, personal experiences, private hopes and fears, feelings about ourselves and others, etc. When any of these data are shared with another person, they then move from **Box B** to **Box A**. **Box B** may be said to represent our private selves or the details about us that we keep to ourselves and don't share with others.

In **Box C** are the data that are not known to us but are known to others. This self is unknown to us until we receive feedback of these data from others. These data might include first impressions we make, behavior char- acteristics we are not aware of (for example, the use of unconscious self- image defenses), positive or negative effects of actions we take or statements we make on others, and any other consequences of what we do. When we obtain these data from others, they become known to us and move from **Box C** to **Box A**.

In **Box D** are the data not known to us or to others. Data found here are below the level of awareness. Therefore, it is difficult to learn anything new about these data. As we become more open, more willing to share the information in **Box B** with others, and the more others are willing to share information in **Box C** with us, the more we know about ourselves and the easier it is to begin to discover some of the data about ourselves that exist in **Box D**.

Reasonable Time And Meaningful Participation

Some people may have an exaggerated expectation of the group experience. They may hope that one or two sessions will provide an immediate personal insight or an instant identity. No group can create self-image awareness or overnight change. Given reasonable time and meaningful participation, however, successful groups can help members develop a more positive self-identity and enhance skills in interpersonal relations. This is particularly true for those who have had limited opportunity to maximize positive social relationships, or to interact openly and spontaneously with others. Only through authentic personal disclosure and self-awareness can we assist ourselves and others in the development of a stronger self-image and an increased sense of self-worth as a person.

Features Of SIM Training

An original feature of SIM Training is the use of a systems model approach to the group process. Group exercises, which have been found to be effective, are provided to accompany each of the training-group functions. The group exercises are included as suggested activities, and the group facilitator may duplicate, modify or add to them to meet individual group needs. It is strongly recommended, however, that group exercises and strategies be used in sequential order to each of the specific functions of the SIM Training systems model. These group exercises and activities, although not all original, have been compiled, organized, modified and utilized by the author over many years as a training-group facilitator.

SIM Training facilitators are encouraged to acquire a working knowledge of the systems training model and communicate this information to program participants before beginning to use the group exercises. Group participants should also be reminded that this is a training course — not therapy. This training is not intended to be a replacement or substitute for conventional psychotherapy or mental health treatment. Though not the equivalent of traditional mental health therapy, the training program utilizes techniques of humanistic education and group dynamics as a means of enhancing participant self-esteem, interpersonal relationship skills and personal human growth.

A summary of the SIM Training systems model is provided in the next chapter.

CHAPTER TWENTY-THREE

Self-Image Modification Training Systems Model

The flowchart in Figure 2 (p. 87) is provided as a guide for SIM Training participants. It represents organizing a system of action for self-improvement and building a more positive self-image. The decision to follow the proposed system, however, can only be made by understanding the potential benefits that will outweigh the personal efforts involved in participating in such a program.

Six Functions Of Building A Stronger Self-Image

The building of a stronger self-image consists of six functions with each function being vitally important to the participants' overall program success.

Conceptualize Self (1.0)

The first function of the SIM Training system is to acquire authentic self-knowledge through conceptualizing the self. Individuals must work to identify both their potentials and limitations. They are asked to focus attention on the qualities and personal assets that they like most about themselves, at the same time keeping an eye on their human deficiencies and limitations. They are encouraged to identify those activities that they are good at — activities they like to do and are interested in, while also recognizing those that they are not good at or are not interested in. The rewards of truly knowing self are the enjoyment and personal satisfaction one receives through the fulfillment of one's true potentials — becoming what one can become.

Group exercises for the first function, *Conceptualize Self (1.0)*, may be found in SIM II, Chapter 26 and the tracking form on page 107.

Statement Of Philosophy (2.0)

After conceptualizing the self, the next function of the SIM Training process is for people to identify and state their philosophy. A philosophy may be defined as a statement of beliefs or values by which one lives. Human growth requires that human beings seek some philosophy or system of beliefs to which they can commit themselves. They must be aware of their values and value conflicts. They need to have the conviction of their values, but also be willing to modify values when values appear to be in error. Personal growth is achieving what one considers to be valuable and important in life, and self-selected values form one's philosophy on which an individual lifestyle is based. Belief in a value system is essential to obtaining self-realization. We each need some system of beliefs to help guide the human growth process.

Group exercises for the second function, *Statement Of Philosophy (2.0)*, may be found in SIM II, Chapter 27 and the tracking form on page 119.

Define Personal Goals And Objectives (3.0)

Defining personal goals and objectives is the third function of the SIM Training system. Program participants are now asked to select personal goals and objectives that will assist them in achieving their potentials and living their values. Goal setting is a major activity in the SIM Training process. When people establish goals and objectives that are specific, realistic, relevant and measurable, they begin to experience increased enthusiasm and motivation required for successful goal achievement.

Group exercises for the third function, *Define Personal Goals And Objectives (3.0)*, are in SIM II, Chapter 28 and the tracking form on page 131.

Evaluate Self (4.0)

The self-evaluation of personal goal effort forms the fourth SIM Training function. Goal achievement can only be realized through personal action and effort. People must evaluate their goal efforts with the knowledge that a sincere desire is the greatest motivator of every human action. The reality of human growth and positive change comes when people apply their potentials and efforts to do those activities that allow them to express and realize their potentials, values, goals and purpose in life. Each must maintain a firm commitment to pursue goal efforts regardless of obstacles, temporary setbacks or difficult circumstances.

Group exercises for the fourth function, *Evaluate Self (4.0)*, can be found in SIM II, Chapter 29 and the tracking form on page 143.

Facilitate Group Support And Feedback (5.0)

Facilitating group support and feedback makes up the fifth SIM Training function. Self-image and self-esteem needs can best be met through participation and interaction with other human beings. The training group is intended to be basically supportive in nature and offers interpersonal learning, feedback and encouragement for those who are in the process of self-actualization, growth and change. Participants' self-images consist of and are derived from the meaningfulness of their relationships with others. The group can provide a viable support system to assist participants in facilitating self-realization and positive self-change.

Group exercises for the fifth function, *Facilitate Group Support And Feedback (5.0)*, can be found in SIM II, Chapter 30.

Complete Training (6.0)

The sixth and final SIM Training function is the completion of training. Unlike many self-help groups, SIM Training is designed for a group closure. Human growth and self-actualization is a lifelong process. Once the group participants have dedicated their energies, talents and potentials to the fulfillment of personal values and goals, the time for the completion of SIM Training is near. By learning to become self-actualized and assuming responsibility for one's own human growth — by continuing to work to achieve one's own potential, each individual will be able to maintain authentic self-esteem and genuine self-acceptance as a worthwhile and capable human being.

Value Of The Systems Model

The structure of the systems model is designed so that an orderly arrangement of the functions provides direction and guidance to program participants. The systems approach to group training is an effective method in providing learning, and reduces the uncertainty and ambiguity of less structured approaches. It gives participants, as well as the facilitator, an understanding of the training process and their role in it. It also provides participants with a systematic course of action leading to desired goals or outcomes, and allows individuals to evaluate their own level of progress in goal achievement efforts. The systems model provides a general structure while remaining flexible enough to consider group participants' individual differences, levels of desired accomplishments and unique potentials for human growth.

The system flowchart in Figure 2 represents a functional system allowing each group participant a free course of goal-directed effort and achievement. By participating in the training-group system, participants will be able to document their own personal inventory of human potentials and limitations, clarify personal values, translate values into goals and objectives, and monitor personal goal efforts in a supportive training-group setting. Since the training system is designed for interrelated stages of human growth, *it is essential that training-group participants proceed through each of the six system functions depicted in the flowchart in sequential order.*

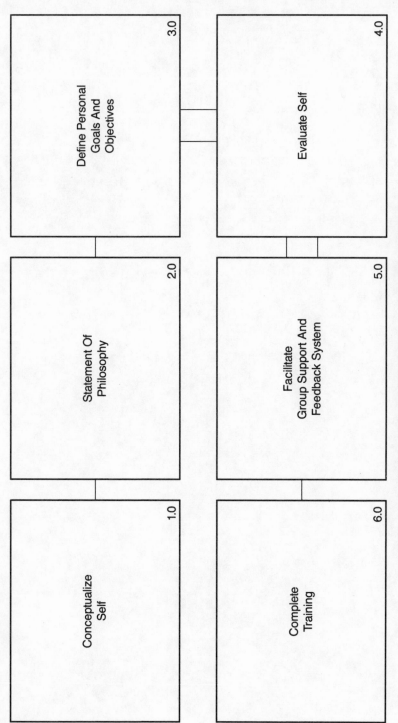

Figure 2. Self-Image Modification Systems Model Flowchart

CHAPTER TWENTY-FOUR

Self-Image (SI) Inventory

Prior to processing the following training-group exercises, each group member is asked to complete the Self-Image (SI) Inventory (see next page). The SI Inventory is an instrument that can be used for examining different aspects of self-image and self-esteem. It is important to remember, however, that self-image is a nebulous factor, lacking specific boundaries or limits, and cannot be measured on any absolute numerical scale. The SI Inventory should be viewed as a subjective self-image indicator rather than an absolute self-image trait assessment.

This inventory also can provide information for self-image awareness prior to starting the SIM Training group and can be used as a post group indicator of self-image change on completion of SIM Training.

In addition, the SI Inventory is provided for each group member's private use and information, and is not intended to be used for open group discussion. All SI Inventory responses are confidential unless voluntarily revealed.

Self-Image Inventory Form*

Our sense of personal adequacy cannot, of course, be measured on any absolute scale. We feel confident about some things, shaky about others. The SI Inventory is designed to help describe how people think and feel about themselves. This self-test is an indication of your self-esteem, your self-perception related to others and your satisfaction with your role in life.

There are no right or wrong answers, and you are encouraged to respond to each statement as honestly as you can. Circle the letter that you feel best fits you. Complete the test and score according to the number scale at the end.

1. In terms of attractiveness, I am:
   a. very attractive
   b. fairly attractive
   c. average
   d. passing
   e. unattractive

2. My personality is:
   a. very interesting
   b. fairly interesting
   c. average
   d. passing
   e. dull

3. I have:
   a. much confidence in myself
   b. enough confidence in myself
   c. average confidence in myself
   d. little confidence in myself
   e. no confidence in myself

4. I think that I get along with others:
   a. extremely well
   b. fairly well
   c. well enough
   d. not very well
   e. very poorly

5. When competing with others, I feel:
   a. I will usually win
   b. I have a good chance to win
   c. I will win sometimes
   d. I will usually not win
   e. I will probably never win

6. I dress:
   a. very well
   b. fairly well
   c. average
   d. don't care
   e. sloppy

7. When I walk into a room, I make a:
   a. good impression
   b. fair impression
   c. average impression
   d. no impression
   e. dull impression

8. I accept personal compliments with:
   a. no embarrassment
   b. little embarrassment
   c. occasional embarrassment
   d. frequent embarrassment
   e. constant embarrassment

9. With the opposite sex, I get along:
   a. very well
   b. fairly well
   c. average
   d. not very well
   e. very badly

10. In terms of maturity, I am:
    a. very mature
    b. fairly mature
    c. average
    d. below average
    e. immature

11. When among strangers, I feel:
    a. very comfortable
    b. fairly comfortable
    c. the same as usual
    d. uncomfortable
    e. extremely uncomfortable

12. I feel warm and happy toward myself:
    a. all of the time
    b. most of the time
    c. some of the time
    d. hardly ever
    e. none of the time

13. If I could make myself over, I would be:
    a. exactly as I am
    b. about the same
    c. slightly changed
    d. greatly changed
    e. another person

14. I experience enjoyment and zest for living:
    a. all of the time
    b. most of the time
    c. some of the time
    d. hardly ever
    e. none of the time

15. I admit my mistakes, shortcomings and defeats:
    a. all of the time
    b. most of the time
    c. occasionally
    d. hardly ever
    e. none of the time

16. I usually feel inferior to others:
    a. none of the time
    b. hardly ever
    c. occasionally
    d. most of the time
    e. all of the time

17. I feel I am in control of my life:
    a. all of the time
    b. most of the time
    c. some of the time
    d. very little of the time
    e. none of the time

18. I have an intense need for recognition and approval:
    a. none of the time
    b. hardly ever
    c. occasionally
    d. most of the time
    e. all of the time

19. When I first meet people, they . . .
    a. like me very much
    b. like me well enough
    c. have an average impression
    d. have no impression
    e. dislike me

20. In terms of body image, I . . .
    a. like myself as I am
    b. like my sex
    c. am not sure
    d. dislike myself
    e. prefer a different sex

---

* Score each question according to these values: a = +2; b = +1; c = 0; d = -1; e = -2. Then total plus and minus points. Subtract to get your score.

** A score of +29 to +15 indicates a PSI. A score of +14 to 0 indicates an acceptable self-image. A score of -1 to -14 suggests a need for some self-image improvement. A score of -15 to -29 indicates significant self-rejection and feelings of inadequacy. A score of -30 to -40 indicates complete rejection of self to an unrealistic self-concept. (**Note:** A score of +30 to +40 might indicate a rather inflated image of self, perhaps as unrealistic as the opposite end of the scale.)

*** The SI Inventory is not intended to be used as a diagnostic test, but represents an inventory for self-awareness and exploration. It provides an instrument for examining different aspects of self-image, and can provide a reference point for self-image insight and change.

CHAPTER TWENTY-FIVE

SIM Training Group Exercises

On completion of the SI Inventory, group members are ready to begin processing the group exercises in the following chapters. These exercises are designed for use by anyone from the age of 16 or older.

Intent Of Group Exercises

The group exercises are designed to assist participants in the self-actualization process and are not to be used as a form of mental health therapy. They are not intended to deal with past psychic wounds or correct serious emotional problems. The focus of the exercises should be primarily on present and future growth issues. The group exercises are to be used in sequence with the six functions of the SIM Training systems model mentioned in detail in Chapter 23 of SIM II (pages 83-85).

Group Size

Since the group exercises vary in complexity and processing time, there is a suggested group size for each exercise that may include large group discussion, smaller group interaction, dyads or triads, etc. Group size is strictly at the facilitators' discretion with considerable latitude in this decision.

Tracking Forms

The exercises are structured and designed to provide the necessary aware-ness and information for the completion of the participant tracking forms found at the end of each function. It is not necessary to process every group exercise, and facilitators will want to pick and choose the exercises that they feel are best suited to fit special group situations or needs.

It is essential that each group member complete the training participant tracking forms at the end of the group exercises for Conceptualize Self, State Philosophy, Define Goals And Objectives and Evaluate Self. These tracking forms provide valuable insight and information that makes personal growth and change attainable. Also allowing for monitoring overall program accom-plishments and outcomes, the tracking forms are designed to provide and document personalized information needed for self-determined goal action and achievement. Though these forms are primarily intended for individual group participant use, information from them may be shared with other group members if desired.

CHAPTER TWENTY-SIX

Conceptualize Self

Getting Acquainted Exercise (1.1)

Function: Conceptualize Self (1.0)

Goal: Personal Disclosure — Being Known

Group Size: Eight to Twelve

Process: This is a very effective activity to be used as an initial closed group exercise.

1. Group members, in turn, are given approximately five minutes to share their life experiences, beginning in early childhood, which they believe have been influential in the development of their personality and self-image.

2. Participants then take approximately one minute to tell why they are a member of this group and what they expect to get out of the group experience.

3. After group participants have completed Steps 1 and 2 above, other group members wanting additional information or clarification may ask participants specific questions related to their personal disclosure.

Self-Disclosure Exercise (1.2)

Function: Conceptualize Self (1.0)

Goal: Self-Understanding — Being Known

Group Size: Unlimited Number of Dyads

Process: During the time given, you are to ask your partner questions
                   from the list. The questions vary in their degree of intimacy
                   and you may want to begin with less intimate ones. Take turns
                   initiating the questions.

Follow these three rules:

1. Your communication with your partner will be held in confidence.

2. You must be willing to answer any questions that you ask your partner.

3. You may decline to answer any questions initiated by your partner.

- What is your favorite hobby or leisure-time interest?
- What do you regard as your chief personality fault?
- What do you regard as your chief personality strength?
- Do you feel that you have a drinking problem?
- Do you smoke marijuana or use drugs?
- What emotions do you find most difficult to control?
- What was your worst failure in life?
- What are your career goals?
- With what do you feel the greatest need for help?
- What was the greatest turning point in your life?
- Do you have trouble sharing feelings with others?
- Do you speak up for your opinions and convictions?
- Are you as sociable as you want to be?
- Can you accept compliments without embarrassment?
- Do things usually turn out the way you want them to?
- Are you able to set goals and achieve them?
- Do you know where you're going in life?
- Do you hesitate to try new ways of doing things?
- Are you getting what you want out of life?
- Do you feel you have a real purpose in life?
- Do you feel that you are in control of your life?
- Is there an area in yourself or your life that you want to change?

Self-Image Sources Exercise (1.3)

Function: Conceptualize Self (1.0)

Goal: Awareness of Self-Image

Group Size: Four to Six

Process: Participants complete and then share their responses to the following statements or questions.

1. Recall your parents or surrogates (substitute parents). In what ways have they affected your self-image?

_____

_____

_____

2. Aside from your parents or surrogates, what other significant person or persons have influenced your self-image, i.e., teacher, spouse, supervisor, close friend, etc.?

_____

_____

_____

3. Recall one experience or event in your life that caused you to feel bad about yourself. Discuss.

_____

_____

_____

4. Recall one experience or event in your life that caused you to feel good about yourself. Discuss.

_____

_____

_____

Turning Points Exercise (1.4)

Function: Conceptualize Self (1.0)

Goal: Self-Awareness

Group Size: Six to Eight

Process: Our self-image can be influenced by significant turning points in our lives. Participants think back to some turning point in their lives, i.e., graduating from school, joining the service, getting married or divorced, taking a new job, retiring, etc. Then they individually respond to the following statements or questions.

1. Identify and describe the turning point experience.

_____

_____

_____

2. Did this turning point contribute in any way to your self-image?

_____

_____

_____

3. Was this turning point a positive or negative experience for you?

_____

_____

_____

4. Did the turning point help you grow as a person? If so, how?

_____

_____

_____

Personal Compliment Exercise (1.5)

Function: Conceptualize Self (1.0)

Goal: Giving and Receiving of Compliments

Group Size: Six to Eight

Process: Practice in giving and receiving personal compliments helps us be more truly ourselves and relate better to others. Group participants are asked to disclose something about themselves that they are proud of, i.e., a personal accomplishment, special talent, etc. After sharing positive statements about self, members of the group are asked to respond with complimental reinforcement statements about individuals' disclosed abilities or potentials. After giving and receiving personal compliments, participants are, in turn, asked to respond to the following questions:

1. Did you feel that the compliments were genuine and sincere?

_____

_____

2. Were the compliments deserved and justified?

_____

_____

3. Did you feel any discomfort or embarrassment in receiving compliments?

_____

_____

4. How did it feel to give compliments to other group members?

_____

_____

5. What were your general feelings about receiving and giving compliments?

_____

_____

Childhood Labels Exercise (1.6)

Function: Conceptualize Self (1.0)

Goal: Identification of Childhood Labels

Group Size: Ten to Twelve

Process: Early in life a child may be assigned a label, either positive or negative, which can influence self-image development. Following is a list of some common childhood labels. See if any of the labels apply to you. If not, think of other labels that you may have acquired from home or school. Discuss them with the group.

Smart	Homely	Reliable
Dumb	Ambitious	Mischievous
Responsible	Lazy	Studious
Irresponsible	Funny	Indifferent
Strong	Serious	Popular
Weak	Generous	Shy
Athletic	Selfish	Cooperative
Clumsy	Honest	Uncooperative
Nice	Devious	Talkative
Spoiled	Talented	Quiet
Cute	Slow	

After identifying childhood labels from this list or from others you have thought of, respond to the following questions:

1. Did the label seem appropriate or accurate to you at the time?

2. Do you feel that this label is still a part of your overall self-image?

Personality Traits Exercise (1.7)

Function: Conceptualize Self (1.0)

Goal: Awareness of Personality Traits

Group Size: Six to Eight

Process: One's personality is made up of many traits. Group participants try to list at least 15 personality traits they like to see in others. The facilitator may elect to begin this exercise by having the group brainstorm a list of positive personality traits.

1. List traits:

_____   _____   _____

_____   _____   _____

_____   _____   _____

_____   _____   _____

_____   _____   _____

_____   _____   _____

2. Participants put an **M** beside the traits they think are part of their personality and a **W** beside the traits they wish were part of their own personality.

3. Participants, in turn, share their personality list, identifying those traits they might wish to include or change in their own personality.

Social Approval Exercise (1.8)

Function: Conceptualize Self (1.0)

Goal: Awareness of Need for Approval

Group Size: Any Number of Dyads

Process: Everyone has a need for approval and acceptance. Gaining approval from significant others can often make us feel good about ourselves while being rejected or neglected can make us feel that we are worthless and that we are a nobody. Participants identify one person in their life, e.g., father, mother, teacher, employer, spouse, etc., whose approval was most important and then tell the group how they felt about getting or not getting this person's approval.

Respond to the following questions:

1. Did **getting** this person's approval in any way affect the way you now think or feel about yourself as a person?

2. Did **not getting** this person's approval in any way affect the way you now think or feel about yourself as a person?

Negative Self-Talk Exercise (1.9)

Function: Conceptualize Self (1.0)

Goal: Awareness of Negative Self-Talk

Group Size: Any Number of Triads

Process: Self-image traits are often influenced and established by self-talk, i.e., what we tell ourselves about ourselves in certain situations. Self-talk may be either negative or positive. We can experience a sense of self-rejection and self-doubt through negative self-talk. Participants are asked to reflect on the following negative self-talk statements or questions and, in turn, share responses with the group.

1. Think of a situation where you made a mistake or experienced personal failure.

_____

_____

2. Recall and describe what negative self-talk you may have used that made you feel guilty or bad about yourself because of the mistake or failure.

_____

_____

3. Without being defensive or making excuses, what positive things could you have said about the mistake or failure that could have helped you think and feel better about yourself?

_____

_____

4. Can you see the specific mistake or personal failure as a positive learning experience that could help you avoid this or similar mistakes and failures in the future?

_____

_____

5. Can you think of some other situations in which you could have changed negative self-talk to positive self-talk?

_____

_____

Looking At Self Exercise (1.10)

Function: Conceptualize Self (1.0)

Goal: Self-Assessment

Group Size: Eight to Twelve

Process: Group members pick a number on the continuum for each
                   statement that best matches themselves. In turn, participants
                   reveal their numbers to the group for each statement. Group
                   members wanting additional information or clarification may
                   ask participant specific questions related to their own personal
                   responses.

1. Can you imagine yourself becoming more successful in some important
   area of your life than you are now?

1	2	3	4	5	6	7
not at all			can somewhat			easily can

2. Are you as skilled and as capable in your occupation as you would like to
   be?

1	2	3	4	5	6	7
not at all			somewhat			very much so

3. Do you have the skills to make new friends and to relate closely with your
   current friends?

1	2	3	4	5	6	7
socially unskilled		somewhat socially skilled			very socially skilled	

4. Does your present work nourish your social and psychological growth?

1	2	3	4	5	6	7
unfulfilling		somewhat satisfying			completely satisfying	

5. Can you be as open and affectionate as you would like to be?

1	2	3	4	5	6	7
inhibited			somewhat inhibited			spontaneous

6. Can you say no to people when appropriate without guilt feelings?

1	2	3	4	5	6	7
uptight			somewhat uptight			easily relaxed

7. Can you relax away your tensions and anxieties?

1	2	3	4	5	6	7
uptight			somewhat uptight			easily relaxed

Conceptualize Self (1.0) Tracking Form

Name _____ Date _____

Potentials And Limitations Inventory

1. The following are what I see as my basic potentials or personal assets:

2. The following are what I see as my basic limitations or personal liabilities:

3. I could take better advantage of my potentials by:

4. I could overcome some of my limitations by:

Conceptualize Self Tracking Form — Notes

CHAPTER TWENTY-SEVEN

Statement Of Philosophy

Value Ranking Exercise (2.1)

Function: Statement Of Philosophy (2.0)

Goal: Clarification of Values

Group Size: Four to Six

Process: Rank the following nine values from the most important to the least important. Place the number **one** by the most important value, the number **two** by the second most important value and so on through number **nine**, the least important value. After each participant has individually ranked values, the group is then asked to obtain a group consensus number, i.e., agreement on one number through group discussion. **Note:** Individual groups may compare consensus rankings.

_____	Money
_____	Love (Affection, Acceptance)
_____	Self-Esteem
_____	Health (Physical and Mental)
_____	Education (Knowledge)
_____	Work (Job Satisfaction)
_____	Leisure
_____	Security
_____	Family

Value Source Exercise (2.2)

Function: Statement Of Philosophy (2.0)

Goal: Awareness of Values

Group Size: Four to Six

Process: Values are learned and may be acquired from many sources such as family and relatives, peer groups, teachers, clergy, advertising media, role models, etc. Participants read and then share responses to following questions or statements. The facilitator may begin this exercise by having the group brainstorm a list of values sources.

1. Review your value system and select two values that are most important to you.

_____

_____

_____

2. How do you think you acquired these values?

_____

_____

_____

3. Were these values freely chosen by you?

_____

_____

_____

4. Were they chosen from alternatives?

_____

_____

_____

5. Do you think your present behavior or actions are consistent with these values? If not, what could you do to bring your behavior or actions more in line with your values?

_____

_____

_____

Philosophy Of Life Exercise (2.3)

Function: Statement Of Philosophy (2.0)

Goal: Clarification of Personal Philosophy and Values

Group Size: Unlimited Number of Triads

Process: Each group member fills out the following Statement Of Philosophy Questionnaire and, in turn, shares responses with group.

1. What do you want out of life?

   _____

   _____

   _____

2. What would it be like to live the life you want to live?

   _____

   _____

   _____

3. What kind of person do you want to be?

   _____

   _____

   _____

4. What contributions would you like to make during your life?

   _____

   _____

   _____

5. How can you translate your philosophy of life into meaningful and achievable goals, i.e., how can you live your philosophy?

   _____

   _____

   _____

Value Clarification Exercise (2.4)

Function: Statement Of Philosophy (2.0)

Goal: Clarification of Personal Values

Group Size: Four to Six

Process: Participants review the following list of values and check 10 that are most applicable to their own value system. Participants, in turn, share value selections. Then discuss what could be done to better live or experience the values that are not presently being realized.

_____ Sociability	_____ Freedom
_____ Companionship	_____ Work
_____ Knowledge	_____ Pleasure
_____ Independence	_____ Health
_____ Security	_____ Cooperation
_____ Love	_____ Decency
_____ Happiness	_____ Personal Appearance
_____ Achievement	_____ Self-Control
_____ Ambition	_____ Self-Responsibility
_____ Assertiveness	_____ Self-Acceptance
_____ Honesty	_____ Self-Confidence
_____ Cheerfulness	_____ Self-Trust
_____ Prosperity	_____ Self-Respect
_____ Leisure	_____ Self-Esteem

Value Conflict Exercise (2.5)

Function: Statement Of Philosophy (2.0)

Goal: Awareness of Conflict Areas in Personal Values

Group Size: Eight to Twelve

Process: Hand out Value Conflict Statements and facilitate open discussion. Have participants add additional value conflicts.

1. You value justice and honesty. You also value money. What would you do if you found a wallet containing an ID and $50 in cash?

   _____

   _____

   _____

2. You value yourself. You also value your friends. How far would you go to do something to deprive yourself to please your friends?

   _____

   _____

   _____

3. You value your health and safety. You also value fun. To what extent would you abuse your body, misuse alcohol or drugs, or risk danger in order to have a good time?

   _____

   _____

   _____

4. You value competition. You also value cooperation. To what degree would you use competition in pursuing your own interests and concerns over cooperation with others?

   _____

   _____

   _____

5. You value your own ideas and opinions. You also value the ideas and opinions of others. How firmly would you stand on your own opinions and ideas over the opinions and ideas of others?

   _____

   _____

   _____

Value Awareness Exercise (2.6)

Function: Statement Of Philosophy (2.0)

Goal: Awareness of Values

Group Size: Eight to Twelve

Process: Group members are asked to identify two objects on their own person that are of value to them, e.g., wedding ring, picture of spouse or loved one, money, credit card, car or house keys, etc. Participants are then asked to say something about each selected personal item, tell how it is seen as a value in their own life and respond to the following questions:

1. Is it necessary to have personal values to live by?

_____

_____

_____

2. Are you presently living your values?

_____

_____

_____

3. Do you feel your values are fulfilling your personal needs and purpose in life?

_____

_____

_____

4. Are you experiencing any personal value conflicts in your life? If so, what are they?

_____

_____

_____

Value Modification Exercise (2.7)

Function: Statement Of Philosophy (2.0)

Goal: Modification of Personal Value System

Group Size: Six to Twelve

Process: Each of us has a philosophy or value system that influences the way we look at ourselves, the world, and the way we think, feel and act. Many of our values are acquired early in life and some may now be counterproductive to our personal growth. We may, therefore, need to modify or change parts of our value system.

1. Participants are asked to identify one personal value that they might like to change. Participants, in turn, share their selected value with the group and respond to the following value questions. (Participants not identifying a personal value needing change may choose to pass.)

_____

_____

2. How do you think you acquired this particular value? e.g., from family, school, church, peers, etc.

_____

_____

3. In what way does this value affect your present attitudes and life situation?

_____

_____

4. What might be a viable alternative value or viewpoint?

_____

_____

5. How might incorporating the modified or alternative value into your overall life philosophy be beneficial to you and/or others?

_____

_____

Value Choice Exercise (2.8)

Function: Statement Of Philosophy (2.0)

Goal: Awareness of Choice of Values

Group Size: Eight to Twelve

Process: Each group member is asked to make an inventory of eight material possessions most valued. The list can include large or small items — a house, a car, a TV, a stereo, a piece of jewelry, etc. They need not be your possessions with the highest monetary worth.

Eight Material Possessions You Value Most

_____   _____
_____   _____
_____   _____
_____   _____

1. Now imagine that, owing to certain circumstances, you can keep only four of these possessions. Which four would you choose and why?

_____
_____
_____

2. As you narrowed your choice from eight to four, what did you have to consider?

_____
_____
_____

3. What conflicts of values, if any, did you encounter in making each choice?

_____
_____
_____

4. Did you have to consider the values of others, i.e., spouse, child, friend, etc., in making your choice?

_____
_____
_____

Irrational Thinking Exercise (2.9)

Function: Statement Of Philosophy (2.0)

Goal: Identification of Irrational Thoughts

Group Size: Six to Eight

Process: Often we are influenced by rigid or irrational thoughts that can stifle our personal growth and self-understanding. A list of some common irrational thoughts or beliefs follows. Which of the statements or thoughts do you hold? If none of the statements in the list applies to you, think about other irrational thoughts or demands you may be making on yourself. Participants, in turn, share responses with the group.

1. _____ You must succeed at everything you do.

2. _____ You must always be right.

3. _____ You must be approved and accepted by everyone.

4. _____ You must be completely sure before you try to do anything.

5. _____ You must be dependent on others and have someone stronger than yourself on whom you can rely.

6. _____ You are completely shaped by your past experiences and events, and cannot change.

7. _____ There is only one right and perfect solution to each of your problems.

8. _____ Life should be completely fair.

Value And Goal Relationship Exercise (2.10)

Function: Statement Of Philosophy (2.0)

Goal: Identification of Value-Goal Relationships

Group Size: Eight to Twelve

Process: Growing toward a fully functioning and self-actualized individual requires the clarification of personal values and the translation of values into goals and objectives. Failing to achieve our values can result in diminished self-esteem while realizing our values through goal accomplishments can enhance self-esteem. Group members are asked to identify and translate one personal unfulfilled value to a goal activity and, in turn, share the value-goal relationship process with the group.

1. Your unfulfilled value is:
   (A value is defined as what you believe to be of importance and worth to you.)

   _____

   _____

2. Your value realization goal is:
   (A goal is defined as a value toward which an endeavor is directed.)

   _____

   _____

3. After identifying a value and goal, each participant is asked to respond to the following questions:

   • Do you really want the goal?

   • Is the goal right according to your value system?

   • Will you be a more fulfilled person when you accomplish the goal?

   • Will accomplishing the goal have any benefit to others?

   • Is your goal legally, morally and socially acceptable?

   • Will you have to compromise any of your values in achieving this goal?

Statement Of Philosophy (2.0) Tracking Form

Name _____   Date _____

Much of your personality and behavior is determined by your philosophy or set of values you have accepted for your personal lifestyle. The function of this philosophy or set of values is to give meaning and purpose to your present and future life.

Write a brief statement of your philosophy that should include values about yourself, your present life, and your wishes for your life.

Set of Values

1. Values I hold about myself are:

2. Values I hold about my present life are:

3. Values I hold about my future are:

4. Other values I hold are:

Statement Of Philosophy Tracking Form — Notes

CHAPTER TWENTY-EIGHT

Define Personal Goals And Objectives

Personal Goal Achievement Exercise (3.1)

Function: Define Personal Goals And Objectives (3.0)

Goal: Identification of Personal Goals

Group Size: Any Number of Dyads

Process: Everyone has experienced goal achievements in life. Participants, in turn, are to share a specific personal goal achievement experience with their partner that they are most proud of. After participants have shared their own personal goal achievement, they are to respond individually to the following questions.

1. What were your feelings about the goal achievement experience at the time?

_____

_____

2. Are you having enough goal achievement experiences in your life today?

_____

_____

3. What goal achievement would you most like to experience next in your life?

_____

_____

After participants respond to these questions, their partner is asked to help them to plan and work out the specific steps they will need to take in order to experience this new goal achievement.

121

Goal Awareness Exercise (3.2)

Function: Define Personal Goals And Objectives (3.0)

Goal: Awareness of Goals

Group Size: Four to Six

Process: Participants read and then share responses to the following questions:

1. Are you satisfied enough with your present life that you feel no further goals are necessary? If not, what personal goals do you consider to be of ultimate importance in your life?

_____

_____

_____

2. Do you feel you have the necessary potentials, motivation and resources to achieve these goals?

_____

_____

_____

3. Are achieving these goals worth the effort, time and energy required by you?

_____

_____

_____

4. How would you feel about yourself if and when you achieve these goals?

_____

_____

_____

Goal Commitment Exercise (3.3)

Function: Define Personal Goals And Objectives (3.0)

Goal: Commitment to Personal Goals

Group Size: Six to Eight

Process: Participants list several activities they would like to do but have not done yet. Then they list several activities they are currently doing that they would like to stop doing.

1. Activities I want to do:

_____

_____

_____

_____

_____

_____

2. Activities I want to stop doing:

_____

_____

_____

_____

_____

_____

Participants pick one **to do** and one **not to do** activity as a personal goal and make a commitment or a promise to self to make an effort to achieve goals. They list some specific steps that might be taken to achieve each goal and make a plan of action to realize these goals. Then they share their responses to these two statements with the group.

Goal Identification Exercise (3.4)

Function: Define Personal Goals And Objectives (3.0)

Goal: Identification of Goals

Group Size: Six to Eight

Process: Participants make a list of steps to take that could make them feel better about themselves.

_____

_____

_____

_____

Participants then respond to the following questions:

1. Are there any of these activities that you would like to commit yourself to doing?

_____

_____

_____

_____

_____

2. What obstacles do you see to these activities and what resources or potentials do you have in overcoming the obstacles?

_____

_____

_____

_____

_____

The participants take turns sharing responses to the preceding questions with group.

Definition Of Personal Goals And Objectives Exercise (3.5)

Function: Define Personal Goals And Objectives (3.0)

Goal: Identification of Goals and Performance

Group Size: Eight to Twelve

Process: By changing the way we act, we can often change the way we think and feel about ourselves. Some negative self-perceptions can readily be changed through minor shifts in behavior.

1. As group participants, you are asked to identify one perception of yourself that you would like to change. For example, "I think of myself as being inconsiderate of others. I would like to change that."

_____

_____

2. You are now asked to think of some possible ways of changing the self-perception. Make a plan to change the way you think of yourself so that you will no longer think of self as . . ., e.g., *inconsiderate of others*, as in the preceding example.

_____

_____

3. You are now asked to disclose to your group the negative self-perception you have chosen to change and describe a plan of action you wish to take in modifying this behavior. Briefly state your plan of action, which should include consideration of who, what, where, when and how.

_____

_____

_____

_____

_____

_____

Goal-Setting Exercise (3.6)

Function: Define Personal Goals And Objectives (3.0)

Goal: Quality of Life Goal Setting

Group Size: Eight to Twelve

Process: Participants answer the following questions and then share their responses with the group.

1. If you learned today that you would die in six months, how would you really want to live until then? What kinds of things would you want to do?

_____

_____

_____

2. What are the most satisfying ways you currently spend your time?

_____

_____

_____

3. How would you like to spend the next four years of your life?

_____

_____

_____

4. What would you really like to achieve in your life? What would you like to become?

_____

_____

_____

5. What goal or goals could you set to enhance your quality of life?

_____

_____

_____

Long- And Short-Range Goal Identification Exercise (3.7)

Function: Define Personal Goals And Objectives (3.0)

Goal: Awareness of Goal Planning

Group Size: Six to Eight

Process: Goal setting involves both long-range and short-range goals. Goal planning should provide a systematic process for goal effort and goal attainment. Goal planning discourages procrastination and allows for a greater utilization of human potential. Following is a list of some common goal areas in life that lend themselves to goal setting. Participants are asked to identify a long- and short-range goal in one of the following or other selected life area.

1. Career Long-Range Goal: _____

   Career Short-Range Goal: _____

2. Financial Long-Range Goal: _____

   Financial Short-Range Goal: _____

3. Family Long-Range Goal: _____

   Family Short-Range Goal: _____

4. Education Long-Range Goal: _____

   Education Short-Range Goal: _____

5. Health Long-Range Goal: _____

   Health Short-Range Goal: _____

6. Leisure Long-Range Goal: _____

   Leisure Short-Range Goal: _____

7. Other Long-Range Goal: _____

   Other Short-Range Goal: _____

When you have completed the identification of long- and short-range goals, make a short-range plan to work toward achievement of your goal and report your planning strategy to the group.

Goal Priority Exercise (3.8)

Function: Define Goals And Objectives (3.0)

Goal: Awareness of Goal Priority

Group Size: Four to Six

Process: Group participants answer the following questions and then share their responses with the group.

1. Do you see yourself as a goal-setting and goal-achieving person?

_____

_____

_____

2. What is your most important goal in life?

_____

_____

_____

3. What is your most important goal priority next month?

_____

_____

_____

4. Where do you want to be one year from now?

_____

_____

_____

5. Where do you want to be five years from now?

_____

_____

_____

Goal Action Exercise (3.9)

Function: Define Personal Goals And Objectives (3.0)

Goal: Implementation of Goal Action

Group Size: Six to Eight

Process: For personal goals to be achieved, a plan of action must be established. The following statements are designed to assist in goal planning and goal action. Participants consider the following three statements and then share responses with the group.

1. Identify several personal life goals that you have already accomplished.

_____

_____

_____

2. Identify one or more goals yet to be accomplished. (It is recommended that no more than three goals be identified at any one time.)

_____

_____

_____

3. Identify specific steps needed to be taken in order to accomplish the goal or goals you wish to achieve. Briefly state your plan of action, which should include consideration of who, what, where, when and how.

_____

_____

_____

Problem-Solving And Goal-Setting Exercise (3.10)

Function: Define Personal Goals And Objectives (3.0)
Goal: Awareness of Problem-Solving Skills
Group Size: Four to Six
Process: Problem solving and goal setting are often interrelated. As individuals, we try to solve problems and set goals almost every day of our lives. Usually there are alternative solutions to a problem. Participants are asked to identify a problem with which they are faced, state the problem and list as many alternative solutions as can be thought of. (Also consider possible outcomes of each alternative.) Participants then share their problems, list of alternative solutions and alternative choices with the group.

1. Your problem is:

   • Alternative Solution: _____
     _____

   • Possible Outcome: _____
     _____

   • Alternative Solution: _____
     _____

   • Possible Outcome: _____
     _____

   • Alternative Solution: _____
     _____

   • Possible Outcome: _____
     _____

2. You have chosen the following alternative: _____
   _____

   because: _____
   _____

After participants have disclosed their problems and chosen alternative solutions, group members may wish to suggest alternative solutions that the individuals may not have thought of. Group members must, however, respect the right of participants to choose their own problem solution goals.

Define Personal Goals And Objectives (3.0) Tracking Form

Name _____ Date _____

Goal Commitment

This establishes my personal goals that I am committed to achieving while participating in SIM Training.

1. My goals are: (Briefly state goals as you understand them to be.)

2. My plan of accomplishing these goals is: (Briefly state your plan of action which should include who, what, where, when and how. Use back of page if necessary.)

3. I plan to accomplish my goal by:

Goal _____
                                                  Day Month Year

Goal _____
                                                  Day Month Year

Goal _____
                                                  Day Month Year

Goal _____
                                                  Day Month Year

Goal _____
                                                  Day Month Year

4. My checklist for goals include:

	Yes	No
Are goals specific?		
Are goals realistic?		
Are goals relevant?		
Are goals measurable?		

Define Personal Goals And Objectives Tracking Form — Notes

_____

_____

_____

_____

_____

_____

_____

_____

_____

_____

_____

_____

_____

_____

_____

_____

_____

_____

_____

_____

_____

_____

_____

_____

_____

_____

CHAPTER TWENTY-NINE

Evaluate Self

Goal Evaluation Exercise (4.1)

Function: Evaluate Self (4.0)
Goal: Evaluation of Self-Directed Goals
Group Size: Three to Four
Process: Participants consider the following factors related to their goal identification, effort and achievement, and then share their responses to the following statements with the group.

1. Self-Evaluation:
   • What are your major potentials and limitations? _____
   _____
   • Are there any areas you really want to change? _____
   _____

2. Goal Evaluation:
   • As accurately as possible describe the goal you've chosen to work toward.
   _____
   • Why did you choose this specific goal? _____
   _____
   • How do you plan to measure your progress toward this goal? How will you know when you have attained it? _____
   _____
   • What factors in yourself, in others, and in your physical and social environment may hinder or help your progress toward goal achievement?
   _____
   • What changes do you expect to be observable to yourself or others when your goal has been achieved? _____
   _____

Goal Procrastination Exercise (4.2)

Function: Evaluate Self (4.0)

Goal: Self-Understanding of Goal Procrastination

Group Size: Eight to Twelve

Process: Most of us often give ourselves excuses for putting off goal action. Participants fill out goal procrastination statements and then share their responses with the group.

1. Identify a personal goal that you have failed to get started on.

_____

_____

_____

2. What excuses or permission do you give yourself for not working on your goal?

_____

_____

_____

3. What are your feelings about the goal?

_____

_____

_____

4. What personal commitments and action steps can you make to overcome your goal procrastination?

_____

_____

_____

_____

Self-Actualization Exercise (4.3)

Function: Evaluate Self (4.0)

Goal: Awareness of Self-Actualization

Group Size: Six to Eight

Process: Self-actualization means to realize human potential through personal effort or action. The goal of self-actualization is to strive to "become the best that one can become." All people have a need to work toward achieving their own potential, to develop talents and attain personal goals. Self-actualization through goal effort and action helps people to gain a sense of personal pride, self-esteem and self-worth. Participants identify a recent self-actualization experience, briefly describe this experience with the group and then respond to the following questions:

1. Did this self-actualization experience help you grow as a person? If so, how?

_____

_____

_____

2. Did this self-actualization experience in any way enhance your feelings of self-esteem, self-confidence and self-worth?

_____

_____

_____

3. The value of self-actualization is the need to do what you are capable of doing — to achieve your potential in order to be fulfilled as a person. Can you identify other areas of self-actualization that could help you more effectively achieve your potential?

_____

_____

_____

Habit Awareness Exercise (4.4)

Function: Evaluate Self (4.0)

Goal: Evaluation of Habits

Group Size: Eight to Twelve

Process: Participants identify personal habits that may be interfering with goal efforts. (This activity may be started by having the group brainstorm the list of habits before the facilitator gives out the Habit Exercise Sheet.) Participants pick one personal habit they would like to change, and then share and discuss it with the group.

1. Major Habits or Routines: Change Desired:

   Work

   Food

   Alcohol or Drugs

   Leisure Time

   Money

   Family

   Health

   Other _____

2. Questions:

   • Would a change in certain habits be beneficial to you?

   _____

   _____

   • What change in habits would make you feel better about yourself?

   _____

   _____

   • What change in habits would help you enjoy life more?

   _____

   _____

   • What change in habits would help you in your goal efforts?

   _____

   _____

Goal Effort Exercise (4.5)

Function: Evaluate Self (4.0)

Goal: Identification of Personal Goal Effort

Group Size: Six to Eight

Process: Being challenged with a new goal can be a richly rewarding
                   experience providing we are able and willing to make the
                   necessary goal effort. Participants are asked to reveal a per-
                   sonally selected goal and then respond to the following goal
                   effort statements or questions:

1. What is your selected specific goal?

   _____

   _____

2. What is happening regarding your goal effort?

   _____

   _____

3. What is not happening regarding your goal effort?

   _____

   _____

4. Do you need more goal effort motivation to accomplish your goal?

   _____

   _____

5. What are the possible causes of your lack of necessary goal effort?

   _____

   _____

6. What kind of a goal effort plan can you make to better increase your goal
   effort?

   _____

   _____

Personal Dependency Exercise (4.6)

Function: Evaluate Self (4.0)

Goal: Identification of Personal Dependencies

Group Size: Four to Six

Process: Excessive dependence on others or things can sometimes make us feel inadequate and extremely vulnerable. One can form dependencies on many external sources including alcohol, drugs, individuals, groups, institutions, etc. Participants identify someone or something on which they feel dependent. They then reveal the dependency source and respond to the following questions. (Those who feel they have no present dependencies may choose to pass.)

1. When your dependency on this source is not satisfied, how do you feel?

_____

_____

_____

2. Does this dependency in any way hinder your personal goal effort?

_____

_____

_____

3. What could you do to overcome this dependency?

_____

_____

_____

Goal Control Exercise (4.7)

Function: Evaluate Self (4.0)

Goal: Control of Personal Goals

Group Size: Four to Six

Process: Goal achievement requires self-direction and self-control. Group participants answer the following questions and then share their responses with the group.

1. Do you usually complete the goals you start out to achieve?

_____

_____

_____

_____

2. Are there any controlling influences in your life keeping you from achieving your present goals?

_____

_____

_____

_____

3. How can you take more control over your life and what happens to you?

_____

_____

_____

_____

4. Can you trust yourself to keep the promises you make to yourself?

_____

_____

_____

_____

Self-Responsibility Exercise (4.8)

Function: Evaluate Self (4.0)

Goal: Awareness of Responsibility

Group Size: Four to Six

Process: Goal effort requires a sense of personal responsibility. Participants are asked to recall three positive life experiences and three negative life experiences. They write them down in the following spaces, and then put an X in front of those experiences resulting from personal responsibility and an O in front of those involving no personal responsibility. Next they share the recalled personal experiences with the group, telling how they did or did not have responsibility for each experience.

1. _____ Positive Experience:

_____

_____

2. _____ Positive Experience:

_____

_____

3. _____ Positive Experience:

_____

_____

1. _____ Negative Experience:

_____

_____

2. _____ Negative Experience:

_____

_____

3. _____ Negative Experience:

_____

_____

Goal Obstacle Exercise (4.9)

Function: Evaluate Self (4.0)

Goal: Awareness of Goal Obstacles

Group Size: Four to Six

Process: In our efforts to reach goals, we may experience certain obstacles that can hinder goal achievement. If we experience difficulty in doing what we want to do, there are usually ways to overcome the obstacles. Participants list their goals and identify what obstacles, if any, may be hindering goal achievement. Then they discuss with the group what can be done to overcome the obstacles.

1. Goal: _____

   Goal Obstacles: _____

   _____

   What can be done to overcome these obstacles? _____

   _____

   _____

2. Goal: _____

   Goal Obstacles: _____

   _____

   What can be done to overcome these obstacles? _____

   _____

   _____

3. Goal: _____

   Goal Obstacles: _____

   _____

   What can be done to overcome these obstacles? _____

   _____

   _____

Self-Image And Positive Self-Control Exercise (4.10)

Function: Evaluate Self (4.0)

Goal: Awareness of Self-Control

Group Size: Four to Six

Process: Positive self-control is very important in maintaining a positive image of self and achieving personal goals. Oftentimes we may feel we are victims, or have little or no control over life circumstances. Group participants are asked to consider and respond to the following questions:

1. Are there things happening to you in your present life that you feel you have no control over? If so, what are they?

_____

_____

_____

2. Are you actively in charge of your own life or just a victim of life circumstances?

_____

_____

_____

3. Are there things going on in your life that lie within your control, either through a change in your social or physical environment, or change in yourself?

_____

_____

_____

4. What other things can you do to achieve your goals or to get more self-control over your life?

_____

_____

_____

Evaluate Self (4.0) Tracking Form

Name _____ Date _____

Weekly Self-Evaluation Check List Of Goal Efforts

These efforts begin as soon as personal goals have been identified.

My Goals	Week															
	1	2	3	4	5	6	7	8	9	10	11	12	13	14	15	16

Mark yourself for your weekly goal efforts using the following scale:
0 = No Effort, 1 = Some Effort, 2 = Good Effort, 3 = Excellent Effort

Evaluate Self Tracking Form — Notes

CHAPTER THIRTY

Facilitate Group Support And Feedback

Self-Image Projection Exercise (5.1)

Function: Facilitate Group Support And Feedback (5.0)
Goal: Self-Awareness
Group Size: Any Number of Triads
Process: All people project a self-image that they may not be aware of. The image people project is an important part of the human growth process. Participants write brief answers to the following:

1. What image do you think you project to others?

_____

_____

_____

2. How and in what way, if any, would you like to improve this projected image?

_____

_____

_____

3. After sharing your self-image statement with your group, ask other members for feedback to this question:
   "What self-image do you see me projecting and how do you think I might improve it?"

_____

_____

_____

Resistance To Self-Change Exercise (5.2)

Function: Facilitate Group Support And Feedback (5.0)

Goal: Identification of Forces Against Self-Change

Group Size: Four to Six

Process: Self-change is a difficult task that is often met with some resistance. We need to identify forces working against change. A list of common factors that can stifle positive change follows. Participants are asked to rank these 12 factors in order of importance. Start with the number one for the most important factor against self-change and continue until a rank has been assigned to all 12 factors. Participants are then asked to discuss their individual rankings when finished.

_____ Unclear goals and objectives

_____ Fear of failure

_____ Fear of success

_____ Lack of confidence in ability to change

_____ Satisfaction with status quo

_____ Lack of understanding about what changes are needed

_____ Failure in planning for change

_____ Inadequate rewards for change

_____ Failure of evaluating progress toward change

_____ Past experience with change

_____ Lack of effort to change

_____ Reaction of other people to change

Personal Disclosure And Feedback Exercise (5.3)

Function: Facilitate Group Support And Feedback (5.0)
Goal: Self-Understanding — Being Known
Group Size: Eight to Twelve
Process: Each participant completes the following Personal Disclosure And Feedback Sheet. (Exercise can be done on separate sheet of paper.) The facilitator collects the sheets, reads a self-description statement and has the group identify who wrote it. The facilitator then reads each participant's group description and asks for group feedback to the participant.

1. Write a brief statement describing the kind of person you believe yourself to be.

_____

_____

_____

2. What do you see as your personal strengths or potentials?

_____

_____

_____

3. What do you see as keeping you from utilizing these strengths and potentials?

_____

_____

_____

4. Write a brief statement describing the kind of person you think the group believes you to be.

_____

_____

_____

5. What do you think the group sees as your strengths or potentials?

_____

_____

_____

6. What do you think the group sees as keeping you from using your strengths and potentials?

_____

_____

_____

Johari Window Self-Disclosure And Feedback Exercise (5.4)

Function: Facilitate Group Support And Feedback (5.0)
Goal: Group Feedback
Group Size: Eight to Twelve
Process: The facilitator presents information on the Johari Window
                  Model (p. 81). Participants fill out the Feedback Recording
                  Sheet. The Feedback Sheet can be cut into strips to be dis-
                  tributed to each participant. (The exercise can be done on a
                  separate sheet of paper.)

Write your impressions of the major personality traits or characteristics of
each group participant in the space below. (The facilitator arranges for
distribution of completed feedback recording sheets to group members.)

Participant   **Traits or Characteristics**

1. _____   _____
                                 _____
                                 _____

2. _____   _____
                                 _____
                                 _____

3. _____   _____
                                 _____
                                 _____

4. _____   _____
                                 _____
                                 _____

5. _____   _____
                                 _____
                                 _____

6. _____   _____
                                 _____
                                 _____

7. _____   _____
                                 _____
                                 _____

Positive Feedback Exercise (5.5)

Function: Facilitate Group Support And Feedback (5.0)

Goal: Communication of Positive Feedback

Group Size: Eight to Twelve

Process: Group participants are asked to write the names of all other group members on the left side of a blank sheet of paper.

1. Then by each group member's name, participants list positive qualities that are believed to best describe that individual, e.g., friendly, sensitive, helpful, honest, kind, etc. At least one positive quality is to be identified and listed for each group member.

2. The group facilitator collects all papers, and reads the name and positive qualities listed for each group member. (The facilitator may choose to have names and identified qualities listed on a blackboard for better group observation.)

3. Group members may be asked to participate in open group discussion on their experience in receiving and giving positive feedback.

Self-Image Validation Exercise (5.6)

Function: Facilitate Group Support And Feedback (5.0)

Goal: Validation of Personality Traits

Group Size: Eight to Twelve

Process: Our self-image is determined by how we think and feel about ourself as a person. It includes the subjective definition we have of our personality traits and can be considered valid if it appears to reflect pretty much what we are, and invalid if it fails to give an accurate or true description. Group participants are asked to disclose their own list of traits on the Conceptualize Self Potentials And Limitations Tracking Form (p. 107) and then they ask the group to give feedback as to the validation or nonvalidation of these traits. Next participants are asked to respond to the following questions:

1. Do you agree or disagree with the group's feedback on your self-description?

_____

_____

_____

_____

_____

2. Does the group generally see you as you see yourself, i.e., has your image of self been validated by the group responses and feedback?

_____

_____

_____

_____

_____

Self-Ideal Exercise (5.7)

Function: Facilitate Group Support And Feedback (5.0)

Goal: Awareness of Self-Ideal

Group Size: Eight to Twelve

Process: The self-ideal, in contrast to how we see ourselves, is the way we would like to be. It consists of our hopes and aspirations for ourselves — the kind of person we wish to be or would like to become. Others whom we respect, admire or see as positive role models can influence our self-ideal. Participants are asked to try and identify three people (living or dead) who have influenced their own self-ideal and then share their responses with the group.

Following are three people who have been positive role models in your life:

1. _____

   Why?

   _____

   _____

   _____

2. _____

   Why?

   _____

   _____

   _____

3. _____

   Why?

   _____

   _____

   _____

Self-Disclosure And Group Feedback Exercise (5.8)

Function: Facilitate Group Support And Feedback (5.0)

Goal: Disclosure of Self-Image And Feedback

Group Size: Eight to Twelve

Process: How we think and feel about ourself as a person — our self image — influences our thoughts, feelings and our behavior, and has much to do with how we respond to life situations. Participants are asked to write a brief self-description — a thumbnail sketch of what they are like as a person. Then the participants are asked to disclose their own self-description to the group and respond to the following:

1. Have you mentioned more positive or more negative traits?

_____

_____

_____

2. Do you have more difficulty in thinking of positive or negative traits?

_____

_____

_____

3. What does your self-description tell you about your self-image?

_____

_____

_____

4. Group members are encouraged to give feedback or validation regarding the individual self-image disclosure.

_____

_____

_____

Self-Image And Stress Management Exercise (5.9)

Function:	Facilitate Group Support And Feedback (5.0)
Goal:	Awareness of Stress Management
Group Size:	Eight to Twelve
Process:	Our self-image, value system and temperament have much to do with how we interpret and handle stress. The following questions provide a self-assessment of stress management. Participants are asked to consider the following questions and then share their answers with the group.

1. Do you get impatient with delays or interruptions?
2. Do you become nervous or anxious when you don't have anything to keep you busy?
3. Do you frequently worry about your safety or security?
4. Are you easily frustrated when things don't go your way?
5. Do you often find yourself lacking confidence in your own abilities?
6. Do you tend to worry about the future or expect the worst to happen?
7. Do you become overexcited or upset when under moderate pressure?
8. Do you feel depressed or angry when you don't perform up to your expectations?
9. Do you have trouble forgiving yourself when you fail or make a mistake?
10. Do you get upset, or feel a sense of personal rejection when people don't agree with your point of view on things?
11. Do you try to do too much at once or spread yourself "too thin" in terms of your time?
12. Do you find yourself frequently over-reacting or getting irritable over trivial things?
13. Do you have little time for leisure activities, hobbies or time by yourself?
14. Do you have a tendency to talk too fast or interrupt others while they are talking?
15. Are you constantly worried or concerned about what others may be thinking or saying about you?
    A way to help cope with stress is to find a stress management activity such as physical exercise, reading, music, meditation, etc.

    What stress management activity, if any, do you find helpful?

_____

_____

Group Closure Exercise (5.10)

Function: Facilitate Group Support And Feedback (5.0)
Goal: Critique the Group
Group Size: Total Group
Process: All during our lives we find ourselves sharing in group
                 activity. Groups can have many different tasks and functions.
                 The training group participants have just completed offered
                 an opportunity to learn more about themselves and others.
                 The following questions are provided to help them critique
                 their training-group experience. Participants are asked to
                 answer the following questions and share their responses
                 with the total group.

1. What did you learn from this training-group experience? What did you
   learn about yourself and others?

   _____

   _____

2. Did you share your knowledge, opinions and ideas with the group? Or did
   you keep your ideas and opinions to yourself?

   _____

   _____

3. Did you encourage your fellow group members to do well? Or were you
   indifferent to their efforts and achievements?

   _____

   _____

4. Do you feel that you experienced caring concern, encouragement and
   support from the group?

   _____

   _____

5. Do you think you have achieved any personal growth and positive change
   from your group experience? In any way do you think and feel differently
   about yourself since participating in the group?

   _____

   _____

6. Would you ever recommend this kind of training-group experience for a
   relative, friend or close acquaintance?

   _____

   _____

CHAPTER THIRTY-ONE

Complete Training

Achieving and maintaining a positive image of self requires that individuals establish the personal life goals that will allow them to become the best that they can be. To become one's personal best is truly the ultimate goal that one can hope to attain. SIM Training, provided in a human environment of understanding and support, produces a powerful source of goal achievement and reinforcement. Though offering no panaceas, the training experience can assist all group members in gaining insight regarding their own self-image strengths and limitations.

When we underestimate our strengths, abilities and unique talents, we are damaging the prospect of fulfilling our potentials just as surely as we do when we choose to overlook or ignore our human constraints and limitations. The SIM Training system also provides a blueprint for translating self-knowledge into action (self-actualization). Self-actualization can provide a strong foundation for building more positive self-image and inner self-esteem.

Premise Of SIM Training

SIM Training is based on the premise that human beings are potentially in the state of becoming more than they presently are, or believe themselves to be, provided they have the self-awareness and intrinsic motivation to do so. Program participants are provided an opportunity for the enhancement of self-image strength. Through the increase of self-image strength trainees may acquire a better feeling toward themselves as well as toward others. Self-image strength, like physical strength, can only be sustained through constant exercise. Exercising both the mind and the body is the key to the self-image building process. It is easy for those who have experienced positive change to drift back where they were when they first started. In order to avoid this regression in the self-image building process, all must be prepared to check themselves out regularly as to the fulfillment of their own personal goals and objectives, and to retain the courage and fortitude to set new goals and objectives as they may be needed.

Outcome Of SIM Training

On completion of the SIM Training program, individual participants generally experience an increase in self-acceptance, self-regard, self-reliance and self-esteem. Some begin doing activities that they previously avoided, or become more willing to take reasonable risks, accept new challenges and make new lifestyle changes. They often state that they assume more responsibility for their own lives, and are better able to work out their personal problems and fulfill their own needs. They frequently become more gregarious and better able to establish more positive social relationships with others. Becoming more flexible and tolerant, and less rigid and defensive are common experiences. Participants are better able to clarify their values, set realistic and achievable goals, and accept themselves as imperfect, changing, growing and worthwhile human beings. They tend to take more pride in what they are, and enjoy and appreciate their unique individuality.

A Continuing Process

Recognizing that many PSI changes can and do occur while participating in SIM Training, it must be remembered that this is just another step and not arrival in the ongoing self-image building and modification process. Once we have discovered our image of who and what we are, we must then accept the fact that change is inevitable. It is important and realistic that we accept who we are in the present, but personal growth means that our needs, values and goals all change with age, new experiences and increased self-knowledge. One's image of self can be continually modified to match one's new standards, values, goals, personal expectations and accomplishments.

Individuals must continue working on their own self-image modification and personal growth. Once they have a positive identity about who they are and what they can become, it is important to maintain effort and self-direction in the goal achievement process. Goal setting and achievement are the keys to human growth. One cannot long sustain this growth without continued motivation and effort to do so. Personal effort, persistence, perseverance and positive attitude are required to achieve and maintain a positive self-image and self-esteem. To assure continued and long-lasting progress in the life journey toward self-esteem enhancement, we must remain alert to thoughts, feelings and behaviors that can contribute to a positive self-image and self-esteem.

Ten Rules For Assuring PSI

These ten rules are for assuring a PSI and self-esteem. Individuals are asked to occasionally review this list, which can act as a conscious reminder of ways to attain factors of PSI that can lead us where we want to be:

1. Like yourself — do not dwell on your faults and weaknesses. Emphasize your good traits and potentials. Keep believing and telling yourself, "I'm good. I have value and worth as a person." Do not feel inferior or acquire a sense of false self-esteem by becoming self-centered.
2. Cope with life problems — do not let problems continue to build up without making the necessary decisions and efforts to solve them. Believe that dealing with your real and often painful problems, instead of using negative escapes, such as alcohol or other mind-altering drugs, will make the problems go away.
3. Satisfy your human needs. Don't be a martyr and suffer need deprivation. Satisfying needs can eliminate feelings of low self-esteem.
4. Accept responsibility and positive self-control over your life. Assume responsibility for your thoughts, feelings and behavior. Believe you have freedom of choice. Do not play the victim role in life.
5. Expect good things to happen — be an optimist — take the brightest possible view of a situation. Believe that the best will happen and that good always outweighs the bad.
6. Heed your values — do not compromise your values of right and wrong. Obey your value system in your pursuit of life goals. Have the courage of your convictions.
7. Set realistic goals — have realistic expectations. Be human. Set goals within reach and invite success.
8. Care about others — look for the good in others. Use constructive criticism. Do not use negative put downs. Do not try to make yourself look bigger by attempting to make others appear smaller.
9. Express your true feelings. Believe you can say what you really think. Don't keep your thoughts and feelings to yourself for fear that others won't accept or like you. Be assertive.
10. Believe that you are not totally shaped by past events and experiences, but that you can change. Avoid feelings of helplessness and hopelessness in your ability to enjoy a happy, meaningful and productive life. Value and appreciate the self-esteem that comes from achieving your potential.

EPILOGUE

The writing of this book has been underway for a very long time and has grown out of my conviction that a systematic approach to building self-esteem could be accomplished. Favorable responses from hundreds of my own SIM Training clients, as well as numerous letters from teachers, counselors, social workers, ministers and others in the helping professions using my program, have been most gratifying. I do not suggest that this program provides a miraculous solution to all human problems, but it has offered an approach which has proven successful in helping many people to start a new way of life and subsequently to feel better about themselves. I do not pretend to have found all the answers to the complex task of actualizing human potential and building self-esteem; but if this work continues to assist others in their search for a more positive self-image, my efforts have been richly rewarded.

BIBLIOGRAPHY

Allport, Gordon W. **Becoming**. New Haven and London: Yale University Press, 1955.

Brande, Dorothea. **Wake Up And Live**. New York: Cornerstone Library, 1974.

Brandon, Nathaniel. **The Psychology Of Self-Esteem**. New York: Bantam Books, 1969.

_____. **The Disowned Self**. New York: Bantam Books, 1973.

_____. **Honoring The Self**. New York: Bantam Books, 1984.

_____. **How To Raise Your Self-Esteem**. New York: Bantam Books, 1987.

Briggs, Dorothy C. **Your Child's Self-Esteem**. Garden City, NJ: Doubleday, 1970.

Canfield, Jack, and Wells, Harold C. **100 Ways To Enhance Self-Concept In The Classroom**. Englewood Cliffs, NJ: Prentice-Hall, 1976.

Centi, Paul J. **Up With The Positive, Out With The Negative**. Englewood Cliffs, NJ: Prentice-Hall, 1981.

Cordell, Franklin D., and Giebler, Gale R. **Take 10 To Grow**. Niles, IL: Argus Communications, 1978.

Dodson, Fitzhugh. **The You That Could Be**. Chicago, IL: Follett Publishing, 1976.

Elkins, Dov Peretz. **Glad To Be Me**. Englewood Cliffs, NJ: Prentice-Hall, 1976.

Frey, Diane, and Carlock, C. Jesse. **Enhancing Self-Esteem**. Muncie, IN: Accelerated Development, 1984.

Frisch, Ann, and Frisch, Paul. **Discovering Your Hidden Self**. New York: New American Library, 1976.

Greenwald, Jerry. **Be The Person You Were Meant To Be**. New York: Dell Publishing, 1973.

Hampden-Turner, Charles, and May, Rollo. **Who Are You?** Englewood Cliffs, NJ: Prentice-Hall, 1974.

Hulme, William. **When I Don't Like Myself**. New York: Popular Library, 1976.

Kennedy, Eugene. **If You Really Knew Me, Would You Still Like Me?** Niles, IL: Argus Communications, 1975.

Lembo, John. **Help Yourself.** Niles, IL: Argus Communications, 1974.

Losoncy, Lewis E. **Turning People On.** Englewood Cliffs, NJ: Prentice-Hall, 1977.

Maltz, Maxwell. **Psycho-Cybernetics.** New York: Warner Books, 1975.

————. **The Magic Power Of Self-Image Psychology.** New York: Pocket Books, 1974.

May, Rollo. **Man's Search For Himself.** New York: Dell Publishing, 1953.

Montagu, Ashley. **On Being Human.** New York: Hawthorn Books, 1966.

Moustakas, Clark E. **Turning Points.** Englewood Cliffs, NJ: Prentice-Hall, 1977.

Newburger, Howard, and Lee, Marjorie. **Winners And Losers.** New York: New American Library, 1974.

Newman, Mildred, and Berkowitz, Bernard. **How To Be Your Own Best Friend.** New York: Ballantine Books, 1971.

Pollock, Ted. **Managing Yourself Creatively.** New York: Hawthorn Books, 1971.

Porat, Frieda. **Positive Selfishness.** Millbrae, CA: Celestial Arts, 1977.

Powell, John. **Why Am I Afraid To Tell You Who I Am?** Niles, IL: Argus Communications, 1969.

Samuels, Shirley C. **Enhancing Self-Concept In Early Childhood.** New York: Human Sciences Press, 1977.

Satir, Virginia. **Peoplemaking.** Palo Alto, CA: Science & Behavior Books, 1972.

Simmermacher, Donald G. **Self-Image Modification Training.** Pompano Beach, FL: Health Communications, 1981.

Twerski, Abraham J. **Like Yourself — And Others Will Too.** Englewood Cliffs, NJ: Prentice-Hall, 1978.

Warner, Samuel J. **Self-Realization And Self-Defeat.** New York: Grove Press, 1966.

Weinberg, George. **Self-Creation.** New York: Avon Books, 1978.

Williams, Richard J. **I Just Met Someone I Like And It's Me!** New York: Sensory Research, 1976.

A GIRL'S GUIDE TO...
MAN MANAGEMENT